ButterflyLiving

Life Changing Stories

A Devotional Collection
Revealing God's Faithfulness
and Transforming Power

Compiled by **Mary Rooney Armand**

Cover & interior design by Typewriter Creative Co.
Cover photo by Cristina Conti
Graphics by Canva

Scripture quotations marked (NIV) are taken from the Holy Bible, New International Version®, NIV®. Copyright © 1973, 1978, 1984, 2011 by Biblica, Inc.™ Used by permission of Zondervan. All rights reserved worldwide. www.zondervan.com The "NIV" and "New International Version" are trademarks registered in the United States Patent and Trademark Office by Biblica, Inc.™

Scripture quotations marked (NIrV) are taken from the Holy Bible, New International Reader's Version®, NIrV® Copyright © 1995, 1996, 1998, 2014 by Biblica, Inc.™ Used by permission of Zondervan. All rights reserved worldwide. www.zondervan.com The "NIrV" and "New International Reader's Version" are trademarks registered in the United States Patent and Trademark Office by Biblica, Inc.™

Scripture quotations marked (NASB) are taken from the (NASB®) New American Standard Bible®, Copyright © 1960, 1971, 1977, 1995, 2020 by The Lockman Foundation. Used by permission. All rights reserved. www.lockman.org"

Scripture quotations marked (CSB) have been taken from the Christian Standard Bible®, Copyright © 2017 by Holman Bible Publishers. Used by permission. Christian Standard Bible® and CSB® are federally registered trademarks of Holman Bible Publishers.

Scripture quotations marked (NLT) are taken from the Holy Bible, New Living Translation, copyright ©1996, 2004, 2015 by Tyndale House Foundation. Used by permission of Tyndale House Publishers, Carol Stream, Illinois 60188. All rights reserved.

Scripture quotations marked (ESV) are from The ESV® Bible (The Holy Bible, English Standard Version®), copyright © 2001 by Crossway, a publishing ministry of Good News Publishers. Used by permission. All rights reserved.

Scripture quotations marked (NKJV) are taken from the New King James Version®. Copyright © 1982 by Thomas Nelson. Used by permission. All rights reserved.

Scripture quotations marked (TPT) are from The Passion Translation®. Copyright © 2017, 2018, 2020 by Passion & Fire Ministries, Inc. Used by permission. All rights reserved. ThePassionTranslation.com.

Scripture quotations marked (NRSVUE) are taken from New Revised Standard Version Bible, copyright 1989, Division of Christian Education of the National Council of the Churches of Christ in the United States of America. Used by permission. All rights reserved.

ISBN 979-8-9888580-0-3 Paperback
ISBN 979-8-9888580-1-0 eBook

Contents

Author's Note

Welcome to a beautiful journey of Life-changing stories filled with joy, gratitude, love and the miraculous wonder of a relationship with Jesus. This devotional collection is over-flowing with hope and promise and I am excited to share it with you!

Thirty-four authors have revealed a moment in their lives where a close relationship with Jesus was the remedy for life's sometimes difficult circumstances.

ButterflyLiving Life Changing Stories was inspired by my blog, ButterflyLiving.org, which was created to share stories of how a transformed life in Christ is possible.

The foundation of ButterflyLiving is found in Romans 6:4, "just as Jesus was raised from the dead through the power of the Father, we too might walk habitually in the new-ness of life."

These heartfelt stories share the joy and possibility of *walking habitually in the newness of life.*

I am forever grateful for the thirty-four writers who said yes and opened their hearts, minds and computers sharing vulnerability, pain, grief and wisdom. I am also thankful for the best editor, Barbara Coots, who is delightful.

Jesus never promised a life without difficulties, but He does promise to guide us along the way, showering us with His presence, love and peace. In Christ, we are overcomers pursuing our greatest mission: shining the light of Christ to draw everyone to Him. My hope is that you identify with and find inspiration and encouragement in these pages.

And be sure to scan the QR code in the book to listen and get to know some of our authors as they introduce themselves via audio.

Blessings from a fellow lover of Jesus being transformed moment by moment,

Mary Rooney Armand

Creator of ButterflyLiving.org

1

A Season of Surrender:
Love and Loss Walk Hand in Hand

By Mary Rooney Armand

> *"What's important is that God makes the seed grow.*
> *The one who plants and the one who waters*
> *work together with the same purpose.*
> *And both will be rewarded for their own hard work."*
>
> ---
>
> **1 CORINTHIANS 3:7-8 (NLT)**

As we stood on the sidewalk, a little girl riding her red scooter stopped abruptly and cheerily said, "Hello!"

My daughter shyly waved and I wondered, who is this golden-haired cutie?

I asked the pint-sized stranger if she was visiting someone in the neighborhood. She enthusiastically responded, "No, I live here," and whizzed off.

Now I was confused. Knowing my neighbors well, I was unaware of any recent home sales or pending relocations, so I shrugged and dismissed the comment.

Little did I know that this brief seemingly insignificant encounter would begin an unimaginable journey lasting for years.

A few days later, I learned the cheerful scooter rider was my neighbor's granddaughter. She had moved in with her grandmother to allow time for her parents to regulate their life and hopefully become whole.

This bubbly seven-year-old quickly became a regular visitor to our home and a perky playmate for our daughters.

We adjusted to a new normal with our exuberant neighbor, who quickly became a constant companion for our family. And several months later, she was joined by her five-year-old sister.

One day our family was informed the girls would be moving to a new home. We were devastated.

We had grown to love these precious girls and considered them a part of our family.

A small sprout of an idea, planted in my spirit but resisted by every other part of me, began to form. I introduced the crazy thought to my husband; certain he would disagree.

"What if the girls moved in with us?" I hesitantly suggested. He looked over with a big smile and said, "I was thinking the same thing ... yes!"

What? I was not expecting or hoping for that answer, but the Holy Spirit won and fear lost.

Although I felt completely unprepared for this assignment, I knew God was calling us to step in and provide what we could.

Sorting through doubt and uncertainty, I found comfort in the words of the apostle Paul in 2 Timothy, "If you keep yourself pure, you will be a special utensil for honorable use. Your life will be clean, and *you will be ready for the Master to use you for every good work*" (2 Timothy 2:21 NLT).

Over several weeks, plans for the girls evolved and changed. After hours of prayer, speculation and discussion, we offered to let the girls stay with us until a permanent home was available.

This unusual plan was not an easy decision, and I experienced a persistent internal wrestle with comfort, fear and control. But ultimately, I sensed God quietly whispering, *would you be okay saying no to these girls when you can say yes?*

Fearfully but expectantly, we opened our home and our hearts ... we were *"ready to be used for good work."*

The moment a green light was shining, our new roommates marched over, loaded with two garbage bags full of their belongings. The girls ran to our spare bedroom and gleefully set up their temporary safe place.

At times, the uncertainty accompanying this decision was suffocating. But several thoughts dominated: *How will this arrangement affect my children, and what if it doesn't work out? What if failure, pain and rejection consume a space that once held hope and promise?*

I could share many details about the emotional and spiritual ups and downs during this time, but this story is about how God transformed me during a season of surrender and change.

Although the girls lived with us for several years, they eventually went their separate ways. We had to release them to others, hopeful that the seeds planted in our home would be watered by new gardeners.

But in this season, we gained wisdom that we learned to appreciate. I also learned that my work for God is not exclusively for me or my family.

God uses us to demonstrate love to those He puts in our orbit, whether for a day or for a lifetime.

When I reflect on those difficult years of plowing and planting, I remember invaluable lessons.

- The willingness to say yes to God and plant seeds in the lives of others radically changed me and my family.
- I learned the true meaning of sacrificial love and the importance of investing in others.
- Difficult seasons can be flooded with the goodness of God. At my wit's end doing *all of the things*—carpooling, homework and just feeding six children—a helper came along to lighten the load.
- When things are out of our control, our trust and reliance on God grows.
- Our relationship with Jesus is fertilized and blooms when we exhibit the spiritual fruit of patience, kindness and humility.

- Love and loss walk hand in hand.
- Obedience does not guarantee a certain outcome.
- Sacrifice is hard, but when you surrender to God, it is extremely soul-satisfying.

This season helped our family get acquainted with the meaning of sacrifice and how it transitions your heart to be less selfish and more like Jesus. We had to adjust but did not suffer by sharing square footage in our home and our hearts.

Over the years I have wondered what lasting effect our time with the girls had on everyone.

One day after grieving and wondering if the hard work of relationship building was even worth it, a beautiful flower was given to me: my daughter read me her college essay.

She shared how the time in her life with two additional sisters molded her to become more like Jesus by helping her grow in empathy and compassion.

You may not immediately see the expected rewards of relationship work. But often, if you look closely, God shows you beautiful blooms along the way when you offer love and plant seeds in others' lives.

*"We ask God to give you complete knowledge of his will
and to give you spiritual wisdom and understanding.
Then the way you live will always honor and please the Lord,
and your lives will produce every kind of good fruit.
All the while, you will grow as you learn to know
God better and better."*

—

COLOSSIANS 1:9-10 (NLT)

Mary Rooney Armand is a writer, teacher, and creator of the faith-based blog ButterflyLiving. Her well-received blog, ButterflyLiving.org, about living a transformed life in Christ inspired this story compilation. Her writing is featured on multiple Christian websites and she is the author of the book, *Identity, Understanding, and Accepting Who I am in Christ* available on Amazon. Besides writing, Mary is a life coach, leads and teaches retreats, and has a Bachelor's degree in Marketing and an MBA. She and her wonderful husband Cory live in New Orleans with their 4 children and 2 dogs! Connect with Mary and ButterflyLiving on Facebook, Instagram, Twitter, or LinkedIn.

2

—

Transformation in the Stillness:

A Journey of Surrender and Healing

By Julie Ademe

I love adventure and enjoy a challenge. My friends describe me as quirky and fun. I thrive when I'm constantly on the move, and I relish a challenge. I am a "7" on the Enneagram scale. Not much slows me down.

But being a 7 also comes with a downside. I flee from my emotions, and I prefer not to acknowledge them. Instead, I bury them deep in the sand and will do anything to keep moving so they don't catch me.

Not the healthiest way to live, but hey, I'm fun.

All was well and good in my eyes until my second cancer battle came at me like a crashing wave, throwing me off balance. I was diagnosed with inoperable cancer in my only kidney. Most people are born with two kidneys, so you have a spare if one fails. But I was born with only one kidney, and now with a rapidly growing tumor inside, I didn't have many options available for treatment.

In just a few weeks, I went from loving change and challenges to living knee-deep in the shifting sands of the unknown. My emotions were coming in wave after crashing wave, and I was tumbling in each one. Why now? Why is this happening to me again? Why God? Why?

Over nine months, my questions gained steam as my husband and I sought a second opinion. We tried surgically scraping the tumor out every six weeks, hoping it wouldn't grow back, and when that didn't work, we researched other options online. And through it all, we continued to pray and seek the Lord's guidance.

Ultimately, no feasible option remained but to remove my kidney, leaving me on dialysis until I stayed cancer free for a minimum of two years. Then the search could begin for a kidney donor. The uncertainty was overwhelming. Where would I find a kidney donor? How long would I need to wait? How would our lifestyle change? How would I live a vibrant life in the wait? Where would I find peace? There were so many unanswered questions, and that's when I noticed God was trying to get my attention. He was starting a new work in my soul.

God was churning something within me as I turned to Him and clung tightly to His promises. In the uncertainty, He showed me I could no longer run from my emotions and find the peace I desperately was seeking while waiting for a kidney donor. But how would I change a behavior I'd had for as long as I could remember?

Deep down, I knew I could no longer run from my flood of emotions. I would break into a million little pieces if I didn't learn to process them. I needed help surrendering and processing my emotions. I needed to learn to be still in the Lord's presence and be authentic with my feelings. I needed Jesus.

Finding Truth in the Stillness

Living on dialysis for nearly three years gave me more opportunities for surrender than I care to admit. Because dialysis physically slowed me down, I had more time alone with my thoughts. In the quiet, I was trying to carry the burden of finding a kidney donor. But in that same silence, God gently helped me realize I could no longer avoid my emotions. In the stillness, He was doing a deeper work in my soul. And as He did, my heart softened to face my feelings with the Lord by my side.

Now I see my years on dialysis as a blessing. God slowed me down so I could no longer run from Him. I needed to allow Him to fight the battles before me. I clung to Psalm 46:10, "Be still, and know that I am God." It became my battle cry as I remembered the ways God had been with me in my first cancer battle.

In the stillness and the waiting, I began looking forward to my daily time with Jesus. Journaling became my lifeline as I openly shared my feelings with the Lord. As I stopped running, I saw the Lord unfold His presence before me. He showed up in places where I find joy and solace. I experienced His glory through a yellow butterfly in my backyard, a glorious sunset, a bald eagle soaring above the lake, an unexpected phone call, a loving touch from a friend, and cards upon cards that arrived at the right moment. Each day became an adventure as I began to look for God to show up in the ordinary moments.

In the stillness, Jesus was transforming me from the inside. He was using my long wait for a kidney transplant in the best possible way. He was using it for my good and His glory. He was showing me how to surrender. As the days passed, I was less likely to run from my emotions as I rested in Him and His timing. I was living with joy and contentment in my circumstances. I was shining for Him!

A little over two years into my journey, God unfolded the perfect gift of a kidney donor. While my donor and I waited for our surgery, God transformed our hearts as He prepared us both for the coming changes in our lives. And when Covid-19 delayed our surgery, we cried together, supported one another and trusted in the Lord's timing. God used the extended wait to strengthen our faith and grow our relationship with Him.

Embracing a New Life

Today I am healthy and genuinely living a new life. God used my cancer and transplant journey to shape me more closely into the woman He sees. He continues transforming me from the woman who runs from pain to the one who faces it head-on with my hand in His. I've learned it's okay to sit in the pain, to experience waves of grief and uncertain thoughts ... but then I must release it all to Jesus.

Instead of hanging on tightly to fear, I have learned it's better to allow God to hold it for me. It's still a learning curve, but as a recovering 7, I've learned not to try to face this challenge alone. I need the Lord at my side to continue to live the thriving life He desires for me. So, no matter my circumstances, every precious day of my life, I want to live with Psalm 118:24 in mind: "This is the day that the LORD has made; let us rejoice and be glad in it" (ESV).

Julie Ademe is a blogger, speaker, and author of *Reclaiming Christmas Joy: 25 Days of Refreshment with Jesus.* She's been married for 34 years and has two sons plus five grandchildren. She is a 3-time cancer survivor and a kidney transplant recipient. As she practiced the art of surrender during her health crises, Jesus helped her understand that joy isn't based on her circumstances but is rooted in the love of Jesus and her relationship with Him. Julie is passionate about helping women encounter Jesus in the ordinary moments of their day. Connect with Julie at julieademe.com, Facebook, and Instagram.

3

—

The Long Road to Freedom, the True Heart of God

By Angie Baughman

"The LORD appeared to us in the past.
He said, 'I have loved you with a love
that lasts forever. I have kept on loving
you with a kindness that never fails.'"

—

JEREMIAH 31:3 (NIRV)

"Take a deep breath in. Hold your breath. Breathe out." I heard the woman's firm instructions, but I didn't understand she was directing them to me.

Where am I?

She began talking again, repeating the words from somewhere unknown. I tried to turn my head but realized I couldn't move. It was too dark to see, but it didn't matter because I couldn't open my eyes anyway.

"Take a deep breath in. Hold your breath. Breathe out." When I awoke this time to her voice, I felt a piercing pain in the back of my head. Could she help me? I tried to call out to her, but I couldn't speak. Something was so wrong.

What is it?

Over the next few hours, as I slipped in and out of consciousness, I would remember pieces of the accident.

I recalled recognizing the car approaching me on the wrong side of the road. I remembered being stuck inside the hot van and waking up briefly inside the ambulance. I recaptured the sound of muffled voices discussing my injuries and making decisions about my care.

Why has this happened to me?

It took a little while for the pieces to come together and make sense, and when they did, the picture they created was one of chaos and destruction.

Our family's vehicle had been hit head-on by a man who fell asleep at the wheel and crossed the center line. We were all alive but faced months of hospitals, surgeries and therapy.

The early days of acceptance quickly changed to days of adjustment, and in many ways, adjusting was more difficult. In what felt like only moments earlier, I had been a woman who expertly kept many plates spinning and multiple balls in the air, and suddenly, they all came crashing down. Others managed me, my home, my children and my professional responsibilities. Life was moving on, but I wasn't a part of it.

Who am I now?

In that place of physical brokenness, God began to answer my questions. And although He did not provide the kind of reasoning that satisfied me, I felt His quiet, gentle presence persistently calling me to remember that He is the "I AM" (Exodus 3:14). The God who was with me before the crash was also the God with me during and after the crash. The way forward would become more evident if I could hold onto that truth.

The next steps were physically painful as my body learned to function again. They were also emotionally painful as I heard God asking me to consider the motivation for my perpetual state of productivity. I had been in a long season of doing, and I equated productivity to purpose.

Even though much of that fruitfulness focused on God and church, it still added up to holding tightly to things of the world instead of setting my heart on things above (Colossians 3:2).

As I allowed God to show me a different way of making decisions, we went back to my teenage years when a teacher at my high school abused me. When our relationship became public, the small town I lived in chose to believe his story over mine, and I left there carrying a heavy weight of shame and rejection. It was a crushing blow to an already fragile heart. It encouraged me to build my life around the carefully delivered lie of the enemy, "Remember, Angie, you'll never belong anywhere."

Because I believed I had little value in relationships and communities, I compensated for my perceived inadequacy as a person with effectiveness in producing. I became the one who organized, led and managed a variety of people and things, motivated mainly by achieving acceptance through tangible contributions.

With the crash, all of that came tumbling down around me, and I faced one of the most important questions I will ever need to answer.

Am I worth something if I can't do anything?

I slowly concluded that yes, I am. I am valuable because God says so, and I am at peace when I agree with Him.

Growing up a pastor's kid, I often lived in a parsonage next to the church. Even as a small girl, I would wander over during the week to sit in the empty wooden pews. I took in the carefully carved pulpits and altar rails. I made soft noises by pressing down the well-loved keys on the piano. I ran my fingers over the words "In Remembrance of Me" etched into the front of the altar table.

In those moments, I felt the love and presence of God deep in my soul. I felt connected to my Creator though I had nothing to give Him but my adoration. Somehow, years and life experiences had taken me far away from being able to receive His love like that. Instead of lifting my head to look to Him (Psalm 34:5), I held it down in shame and determination to keep working. But now He opened my heart again to a truth I'd claimed so long ago: I am lovable because my Father says so.

I've heard fascinating stories of people who experienced transformation in the blink of an eye. My story doesn't read like that. It took a long time for me to change from a little girl in an empty, sanctuary relishing the love of her Father, to an overwhelmed woman trying to prove her worth with accomplishment.

The miles taking me back to where I began were long, too. But God accompanied me on the journey, and along the way, He would point things out He wanted me to see. We would stop sometimes and sit for a while as I learned something new. Then we would get up again, hand in hand, and resume our walk.

It seems crazy now to talk about my gratitude for the crash. When I woke to the sound of the woman performing the MRI, I would never have dreamed I would someday say the experience was the best thing that ever happened to me. But I didn't know then what I know now. The crash led me back to the true heart of God, and following that path, I learned to live transformed, loving Him more deeply and myself more fully.

Angie Baughman is a pastor, Bible teacher, author, podcaster, founder of Steady On ministries and creator of the Step By Step Bible study method. Knowing and living by the promises of God helped free Angie from layers of shame, and she now helps others by teaching and testifying to the faithfulness of God in the painful places of our lives. Angie's Bible studies include *A Journey Worth Taking: Exploring the Significance of the Gifts the Wise Men Brought to Jesus* and *Strong Hearts: Increasing Our Trust in Jesus Through Examining the Lines of the Lord's Prayer.* Connect with Angie at livesteadyon.com, Linktree, Facebook, Instagram and YouTube.

4

—

When We Don't Know if We Will Be Healed:

Believing We are Worthy of God's Goodness

By Becky Beresford

> *"Jesus told him, 'Stand up, pick up your mat, and walk!' Instantly, the man was healed!"*
>
> —
>
> **JOHN 5:8-9 (NLT)**

I was lying in bed, still trying to breathe through the pain. I hadn't slept well the night before, like hundreds of nights before that. Asking God to heal me seemed like a never-ending request that was met with the simple but profound, "I am with you."

But that morning was different. An unusual word kept coming to mind, one initiated by the Spirit because I rarely use it.

EXCESS.

God continued to whisper the word to my heart, but I didn't understand what He meant. Was my stomach in pain because I ate too much of something? Was the time I spent on social media exceeding a healthy dose? Was He talking about the overwhelming amount of stress I was wading through because of writing deadlines, fighting kids, financial strife or marital tension? Life seemed like a heavy load. Did He want me to get rid of the excess weighing me down?

Later that day I asked my husband to pray for me, but before he did, I felt like I needed to tell him about this mysterious word that kept floating around in my mind.

"Babe, I keep hearing God tell me the word EXCESS." We googled the definition quickly.

Merriam-Webster defines excess as "more than the usual, proper, or specified amount."

"That's what I thought," I said to him. But then he began to pray something that completely shifted my perspective.

"God, I pray you fill my wife with more of You. More of Your goodness. More of Your love. More of Your healing." And that's when I began to lose it.

Warm tears fell down my cheeks as I began to realize the Lord wasn't necessarily telling me to rid my life of things that were not beneficial to my wholeness and walk with Him (although that is a good idea too). Instead, God wanted me to experience His excess—His abundance surpassing what is necessary or specified in earthly terms.

Paul's words to the church at Ephesus flowed through my mind: "Now to Him who is able to do exceedingly abundantly above all that we ask or think, according to the power that works in us, to Him be glory in the church by Christ Jesus to all generations, forever and ever. Amen" (Ephesians 3:20-21 NKJV).

God wanted me to receive and expect His abundance, whatever that may look like in my life.

But somewhere deep inside was a little girl who didn't believe she was worthy of God's wealth of kindness. In some wounded part of my soul, I still couldn't receive my complete acceptance in Christ. I couldn't grasp how a woman like me, who continues to struggle with sin, could be worthy of more than the bare minimum of blessing.

The compounded effect of comparison to others didn't help. Many wonderful people who were "better" Christians than me deserved to have their prayers for healing answered, according to my evaluation. But our assessment doesn't match God's economy of grace. Sometimes when we look at the needs of others, we can downplay our own. We place ourselves in second class because holier people should get more help and healing.

Except, that's not the way Jesus does things.

In a bold, counter-cultural way, Jesus healed the imperfect, the seeking and the searching. He didn't require suffering people to get their act together before He would save them. He came to be their Messiah, to offer forgiveness, to restore mankind to God. He even performed miracles for those He knew would reject Him.

God doesn't heal based on our actions. He heals based on His purpose and heart.

In John 5, we read about a man who had been sick for 38 years. Every day he lay with other sick people at a pool of water, hoping for healing. Jesus intentionally approached this man and asked him if he wanted to be well. It seems like an obvious answer—yes!

But Jesus wasn't talking about the man's want, He was talking about his willingness. Was this man struggling with shame similar to mine, believing the lie that he wasn't worthy of healing? Was he looking around at the others who probably "deserved" miracles more than he? Now Christ was standing before him, asking if he was willing to let God exceed the expected outcome he had played out in his mind day after day. Was he looking around at the others, thinking everyone deserved miracles except him?

Sometimes we normalize our pain, whether it's physical, emotional, mental or spiritual. We believe it will always be a part of our life because hope has been deferred for far too long. When our prayers are not answered the way we expect, we wonder if God hears us or, even worse, if He doesn't want to offer us His healing. We begin to think we are the problem.

This is Satan's territory, Dear Reader. The enemy slips into these places of pain and persuades us to believe we are to blame. And if it's not us, God is the culprit. He's not faithful. He's not honest. He's not loving because who would let their child endure such hardship and suffering?

Yet, the story of the gospel shows us this is exactly what the Father did.

God allowed His only Son to endure one of the most agonizing deaths created in man's cruel imagination. He let His Beloved die in exchange for the redemption of the world. But Jesus still prayed for the cup to pass. He petitioned the Father for another way. Christ understands the depths of hope deferred, but He also knows the certainty of God's coming healing.

Because Jesus died on the cross, everlasting healing is available to humanity.

Even if healing doesn't happen according to our timeline or technique, we are promised restoration and wholeness in Christ. Whether we wait a few hours, 38 years or until we see Jesus face-to-face, God promises to heal the ailments that make our bodies and souls ache.

But we don't need to wait for physical healing to be healed in our hearts. We don't need to experience the miracle to know the Miracle Maker. He is with us now, asking if we would like to receive His excess that goes beyond anything we could think or need.

Jesus looked at the lame man and listened to his response to His question. The last thing the man said to Jesus is "Someone else always gets there ahead of me" (John 5:7 NLT). Do you know what Christ's response is to this imperfect and honest answer?

"Jesus told him, 'Stand up, pick up your mat, and walk!' Instantly, the man was healed!"

It doesn't matter if we have perfect faith. God is abundantly faithful to bring about His purpose and promises. Our Savior tells the man to stand up and walk before he received physical healing because Jesus invites us to believe God can still do the impossible. Today, regardless of the healing we seek, God wants to bind up our broken hearts and tear down the lies the enemy has tied to our trials. Jesus is asking if we're willing to deem ourselves worthy because God's excess never runs out for His children.

We will receive His healing. And on that day, we'll pick up our mat as a testimony of His goodness ... and walk.

Becky Beresford lives in Chicago, outnumbered by her husband and three wonderful boys. She is a writer, speaker and coach with a master's certificate in discipleship from Moody Theological Seminary. Her first book with Moody Publishers is scheduled for release in March 2024. Connect with her at BeckyBeresford.com, where she hosts the weekly Brave Women Series, featuring different women and their journeys toward courage with Jesus. Sign up to receive inspiring stories in your inbox and a free copy of The Brave Woman Manifesto: Five Things to Tell Yourself When Life Gets Hard. Connect with Becky on Instagram, Facebook and Twitter.

5

When God Says "No"

By Collene Borchardt

*"My health may fail, and my spirit may grow weak,
but God remains the strength of my heart;
he is mine forever."*

—

PSALM 73:26 (NLT)

E verything was going according to plan. I had a loving husband and three adorable children. I had a good job, big dreams and a beautiful vision of what I thought my future would look like.

Life was great ... until everything changed.

One fateful day I turned around to grab something when suddenly it felt like the ground shifted beneath me. I quickly sat down so I wouldn't pass out from feeling so unsteady. But the feeling went away, so I didn't think much about it.

However, over the next few weeks, the peculiar sensation kept coming back. And I started experiencing other weird symptoms like dry mouth, sweaty feet, flushed cheeks, lightheadedness, nausea, heart palpitations, headaches and migraines.

Up until then, I'd been healthy and active. Walking or running a couple of miles three to four times a week. But now, just walking up a flight of stairs left me winded and dizzy. I didn't understand what was happening. So, I saw my doctor. And she seemed just as confused as I was.

That was the beginning of an 18-month journey in search of answers. After many grueling treatments and tests, I was referred to a neurologist, who diagnosed me with the hyperadrenergic subtype of POTS (postural orthostatic tachycardia syndrome), a blood circulation disorder. My autonomic nervous system wasn't working right causing me to experience all of those strange symptoms after trying to stand or walk for extended periods.

At first, I felt relieved. I had an answer. A reason for the bewildering symptoms plaguing me.

But then the neurologist said five words that changed my life forever.

"It is a chronic condition."

This meant it would never go away. I couldn't fix it. Or change it. I'd always struggle with physical limitations. This was my new normal. This was my life now.

I went from being able to walk a couple of miles to barely being able to walk around my block. From working full-time at home while homeschooling ... to working part-time and putting my kids in school.

One day my son came home from school and excitedly shouted, "We're going to the zoo!" But then his smile faded as he continued, "I was going to ask you to chaperone, but that would be too far for you to walk."

My heart broke into a million pieces over the precious moments being taken away from me. It felt like this syndrome was ruining everything. But I knew I served a big God who could do anything.

So, I prayed for healing.

I went to the elders of the church, who anointed me with oil and prayed over me. I asked everyone I knew to pray for my healing. I did everything I thought I was supposed to do. I had faith. I believed God could heal me. But the years passed by ... and He didn't. And I didn't know what to do with that.

A Crisis of Faith

For a while, I struggled with my faith. I grew depressed, bitter and angry. I just couldn't understand why a good God who loved me would allow this suffering.

Then one day I read Luke 22:42, where Jesus prays, "Father, if You are willing, remove this cup from Me" (NASB).

And the Bible goes on to say Jesus was in agony, and His sweat became like great drops of blood falling down. This clearly shows Jesus was quite distressed over this prayer request.

As I read these verses, I realized something. Jesus poured His heart out to God. Pleaded and begged God to answer His prayer. To put an end to His suffering.

And God said, "No."

This was a very humbling realization for me. Even one of Jesus's prayers wasn't answered the way He wanted it to be.

But God didn't say no to Jesus and then walk away. God sent an angel from Heaven to strengthen Him (Luke 22:43). And God had a good reason to say no. Because without Jesus going to the cross ... He couldn't save us.

Considering these things got me thinking. For so long, I'd had my fists clenched around my dreams. My plans. My ideas for what my life should look like. But what if God's plans looked different?

Could I believe God had good plans for me, even if those plans did not include my healing? Could I trust that just like with Jesus, God would strengthen me and use my suffering for good?

God Became My Strength

After much reflection, I asked God to help me surrender to His plans for me. And as I slowly moved toward Him in my disappointment and pain, my season of suffering became like a steroid shot for my faith.

While I'd always gone to church, I'd just been going through the motions. But now, I sought God with my whole heart (Jeremiah 29:13).

Because I knew I'd drown in the emotions of what I was facing if God didn't help me.

And then I came across this verse: "My health may fail, and my spirit may grow weak, but God remains the strength of my heart; he is mine forever" (Psalm 73:26 NLT). The word for strength in this verse is the Hebrew word *sur*. This word can also be translated as "a rock or boulder."

I love that this word for strength can also mean a rock. Because God showed me that He was the only Rock I could stand on. Not my plans, hopes, dreams, health or anything else. Only God could be the strength I needed as I learned how to live well with this condition.

And as I leaned into this truth, the moments when I felt the weakest physically became the moments I felt the strongest spiritually. The days I was stuck on the couch because I couldn't do anything without feeling dizzy became the days I enjoyed the sweetest moments with my King.

And I wouldn't trade those moments for anything. Even better health.

I went from stubbornly clinging to all my hopes, plans and dreams to cherishing an illness that brought me to my knees in surrender before the King of Kings.

God used my poor health to cultivate a rich faith in me. To teach me to stop focusing on what I do and focus on being in a love relationship with Him. To stop seeing my limitations as a disability and start seeing them as a God-ability. Because when I'm weak, the strength of my God can be seen most clearly (2 Corinthians 12:10).

And then God called me to start writing and speaking—things this shy, fearful and introverted girl never would've considered before.

But after going through what I went through, and seeing what God can do ... I want nothing more than to encourage everyone with this truth: even in the most awful moments of life, God is still so, so good.

Even when our world falls apart, God is holding on to our hearts. He's in control, even when everything feels out of control. He knows so much more than we do about what we're going through. And He loves us more than we could possibly imagine.

So, we can trust Him. Even when He says "No."

Collene Borchardt is a speaker, blogger and guest writer who helps women learn to trust God even when life is hard. She is a wife and mother of three adventurous children and three crazy dogs. As a chronic illness warrior and former prodigal daughter, Collene will inspire you to see the good, lean into hope and live for more in your walk with Jesus. Connect with her at RichFaithInPoorHealth.com or ColleneBorchardt.com.

6
—

Trusting God with a Broken and Shredded Heart:

Walking Out of Grief

By Robyn Rison Chapman

> *"And if the Spirit of him who raised Jesus from the dead is living in you, he who raised Christ from the dead will also give life to your mortal bodies because of his Spirit who lives in you."*
>
> —
>
> **ROMANS 8:11 (NIV)**

A pop tart and a glass of wine. That was the final straw.

I had let myself be buried alive. Oh, not in a scary movie way. But after what felt like years of relentless grief and a long list of unhealthy choices. That night, in the weeks following my dad's death, I was sitting on my couch having that questionable dinner when God pressed on my heart that it was time to make a choice. A choice between life and death. A choice to get up and really follow Him.

I grew up in fortunate circumstances, with stable parents who stayed together and made sure that the family was active in the church. And they largely lived their beliefs at home; they weren't any different at home than they were at church. My parents always served in some capacity. It felt like we were always there, at church.

I gave my life to Jesus as a young teenager. I knew all the hymns, all the Bible stories and all the Sunday School answers. I knew that the pastor had a short sermon when he called on certain saints to pray. I knew all the right things to say and do. I was well-churched. But well-churched and $3 will buy you a cup of coffee. By itself, it doesn't mean much. Church never died for anyone.

It was so routine that it was as if I was sleepwalking. I just followed the churchy blueprint and coasted along. Oh, I did some serving from time to time and got out of my comfort zone more than once, but nothing rattled my cage as grief did later. It's easy to get buried when you're not really awake.

In Luke 22 just before being arrested, Jesus is praying and then finds His disciples sleeping. Luke says they were "exhausted from sorrow." That's where I was. Two years prior to my mother's death, she learned her diagnosis was terminal. Other family members and close friends died. I had children after mom died, and while those were joyous occasions, they came with an underpinning of grief for relationships that would never be.

Grief is a tricky business. Jesus grieved. He showed us that it's right and acceptable to grieve. However, I let it call the shots, and it became a grave of its own. I made all sorts of mistakes. I did things I knew were wrong, blamed it on grief and gave myself a free pass.

My entire identity became tied to death and grief when it should have been tied to my Savior. I was stuck in the pain, the unfairness and the limits of my own strength. I knew better but was buried so deep that I couldn't escape it.

He Gave Me Instructions

Twelve years and a lot of hurt and grief later, my dad died. It was different from Mom's death in many ways, but the most noteworthy was that it was the time when the Lord came to me and said, "Get up." I don't know why He chose that way and that time. Mercy comes to mind. But when grief and sorrow were absolutely threatening to consume me, He rescued me.

He began a resurrection and transformation process in me that changed my entire life trajectory.

I often think about Joshua in the time shortly after the death of Moses. In Joshua 1:1-2 (NIV), we see the Lord come to Joshua: "After the death of Moses the servant of the LORD, the LORD said to Joshua son of Nun, Moses' aide: 'Moses my servant is dead. Now then, you and all these people, get ready to cross the Jordan River into the land I am about to give to them—to the Israelites.'"

Joshua surely grieved Moses—his friend, his mentor, a bit of a father figure. Perhaps he felt as I did. Like he wasn't ready to keep going and figure out life without him. Joshua had kingdom work to do, and so did I. The Lord repeatedly told Joshua to be strong and courageous. Those qualities would be needed to face the battles he had coming up, but they would also be needed to turn loose of the past and Moses, whose job was done.

My parents were gone, but I wasn't. I had work to do. I could no longer stay buried in my darkness. It was time to be strong and courageous, to get up, to do the work God had for me. It was time to trust my broken and shredded heart to Him.

He Gave Me Words

He asked me to write from that broken heart, and as I did, He began to transform it. He asked for one story of my grief. Every word brought more healing. Every word seemed to draw me closer to Him. At first, He directed me to start a blog just to house the initial story. Then came post after post. It was like He turned on a faucet, and I couldn't stop.

Then He asked for a book!

My words have now been viewed by thousands of people all over the world. I wrote a devotional book that continues to reach people. It sold better than expected, and I won an award. My devotions run daily on a local radio station. I've been interviewed by radio stations, newspapers and podcasts, and I've written for numerous other websites. I continue to receive speaking engagements at church and women's events.

And I didn't plan or dream a single word of it.

He Gave Me New Life

The entire trajectory of my life was transformed because when I was buried alive in grief, God said, "Arise, get up out of that grave, there's work to do!" I did, and I can't go back. I had a fresh encounter with the Lord and will never be the same. Though I had known Jesus for most of my life, it wasn't until this time that I began to truly experience a deep relationship with Him. It's a new life.

I will miss my parents, and others who have passed, forever, but my race here isn't finished. And, sweet friend, your race isn't finished either—even if you're exhausted from sorrow and you've lost so much it feels like you might be dead, too. We must keep showing up because God isn't finished with us. We must be willing to courageously step out in faith and let Jesus transform us.

Jesus did not defeat death to leave us behind, or hopeless, or to struggle in the darkness and be half dead. We may feel that we are buried alive, but He does not leave. His resurrection power means we can live an abundant life full of hope and joy right now.

Jesus always brings life from death, beauty from ashes, and transforms our brokenness into something gloriously whole and good. He can do the same for you.

Robyn Rison Chapman was once an award-winning journalist and successful grant writer. During a season of family grief, she began to feel God calling her into more faith-filled writing. She is the author of the devotional book, Ordinary Walks With An Extraordinary God, and writes on her blog, www.hopeanyway.com. Her devotions run on WEMM radio.

She has made guest appearances on podcasts and is a speaker at church and women's events. She is the 2023 Best Author/Writer recipient from the Appalachian Arts and Entertainment Awards. Robyn lives in Ohio with her husband, Derek, and sons, Jack and Max. Connect with Robyn on Facebook and Instagram.

7

The Beauty of Weakness in Christ

By Heather Chapman

> *"Therefore I take pleasure in infirmities,*
> *in reproaches, in needs, in persecutions,*
> *in distresses, for Christ's sake.*
> *For when I am weak, then I am strong."*
>
> ---
>
> **2 CORINTHIANS 12:10 (NKJV)**

The ambulance doesn't come in real life as it does in the movies. It takes a long time. You stand there scanning the road and straining to hear the sound of a siren. The drive to the hospital isn't fast and furious either. You aren't met with heroic doctors that work miracles and everyone rejoices at the life that has been saved.

No one prepares you to watch your daughter dying on the side of the road or tells you how to live life when God takes your only little girl from you. I did not truly know fear until that warm summer day.

There is a period of time in which you are sure you've died too, but everything seems to be going on around you normally. Your baby takes his first steps, you still go to the grocery store to buy milk, and your neighbor's cat continues to sit on your doorstep.

How is it possible that the sun shines on the day you put the child you carried inside of you for nine months into the cold, dark ground? As you celebrate the birthdays of your other children, your mind screams to you that your daughter will never have another one. Eight years was all she was given.

She will never turn 13, graduate from high school or have children of her own. She will never giggle with her friends about boys, wear make-up or walk down the aisle on her father's arm.

I am not going to hold your hand and give you an uplifting speech about the goodness of God here. I want you to feel every heartbreaking word, your own pain erupting within you to the point that tears are streaming down your cheeks. I want you to hold back gut-wrenching sobs.

Why? Because this is when you are at your weakest. This is the point at which you feel your humanity at such a magnitude that you despise it. This is the moment we cry out to God. Paul tells us of his secret struggle and how he came to God three times begging for His help.

"Concerning this thing I pleaded with the Lord three times that it might depart from me. And He said to me, 'My grace is sufficient for you, for My strength is made perfect in weakness.' Therefore most gladly I will rather boast in my infirmities, that the power of Christ may rest upon me. Therefore I take pleasure in infirmities, in reproaches, in needs, in persecutions, in distresses, for Christ's sake. For when I am weak, then I am strong" (2 Corinthians 12:8-10 NKJV).

This is where God enters the story. If I have learned anything from the last five years, it is that I cannot do life on my own. I am not strong enough to handle the pain, grief, fear of losing another child, and anxiety that rules my life. It is too much for me.

People would tell me how strong I was, but they didn't see me on the days I couldn't get out of bed. They didn't see me lying awake at night, unable to remove the memories from my exhausted mind. There was no strength there, only emptiness.

Nor did they hear that I cried out to God dozens of times a day because I thought I was losing my mind. They didn't see me sobbing on the floor like a broken child, clinging to the love God had shown me my entire life as if it was my only salvation. (It WAS my only salvation.)

However, much more was going on that even I couldn't see. I didn't see God cradling me, but I could feel Him. No one saw Him plant a seed of faith in me, but I can testify that it has grown into a beautiful flower. God didn't allow me to see His angels touch my cheek as I cried myself to sleep, but I am certain I was not alone.

When did Jesus cry? When He was at the tomb of his dear friend Lazarus. Tears did not fall because His friend had died, but because He felt the pain and sorrow of those crying around him. He knew he was about to raise Lazarus from the dead—a huge testament to who He was and a foreshadowing of His own resurrection. Yet He wept. He was so touched by the humanity of the crowd that His sorrow overflowed. I can proclaim without a doubt that my own tears touched Heaven as well.

I have another verse for you. One I didn't understand until I experienced it myself:

"Most assuredly, I say to you, unless a grain of wheat falls into the ground and dies, it remains alone; but if it dies, it produces much grain. He who loves his life will lose it, and he who hates his life in this world will keep it for eternal life. If anyone serves Me, let him follow Me; and where I am, there My servant will be also. If anyone serves Me, him My Father will honor" (John 12:24-26 NKJV).

When the pain of this world destroys us, we have two choices:

1. We can allow it to make us bitter and angry. We can blame God, other people—and even ourselves.
2. We can die and allow God to raise us up again in His strength and love and peace.

If ever a transformation is seen, it is when we die to ourselves and live again in the beauty of a spiritual world. True love is accepted without question because we are so broken that we are no longer holding onto the selfish love we once possessed. Mercy and grace flow from us because we cling to them knowing that we could not possibly live a day without them.

When we die the death of our own weakness, we live again in the strength and beauty of a life with purpose. Our new purpose is to tell the story of Jesus and His love for us because we know we couldn't have gotten through the pain without it.

Therefore, having died along with my daughter that horrible day in August, I can testify of the beauty of accepting my weakness and clinging to His strength. May the pain this fallen world has handed you allow you to embrace your weakness and cling to His strength. I pray the death you are experiencing leads to a beautiful resurrection as you seek His face and allow Him to transform you into His image.

Heather Chapman is a mom of five, homeschooler, homesteader and lover of all things chocolate. Heather's website, www.lessonsfromhome.co, is a valuable resource if you are looking to grow your faith, heal from loss, or find homeschool resources or inspiration in raising godly children. You can join the Lessons from Home family and receive encouraging weekly emails. You will also have access to many inspirational and homeschool printables. Connect with Heather on her website, Instagram or Facebook.

8

—

Nothing Separates Us From the Love of God:

Miracles Still Happen

By Ginger Moskau Cress

"For I am convinced that neither death, nor life, nor angels, nor principalities, nor things present, nor things to come, nor powers, nor height, nor depth, nor any other created thing will be able to separate us from the love of God that is in Christ Jesus our Lord."

—

ROMANS 8:38-39 (NASB)

I suddenly sat up gasping for air. Sweat poured off my forehead. My heart was racing.

I looked around the dark room and saw the outline of our bedroom furniture. I heard the low hum of my husband's CPAP machine as he slept next to me. Slowly I realized that it was just a nightmare. The dream of being locked into a wooden box, coffin-like, in complete darkness and alone. No one near me, no one to hear my cries. Barely able to move.

I'd never considered myself claustrophobic, yet this vivid dream created a sense of panic I'd never experienced. Over the next few days, I recalled the dream, and it still drew me back to a place of terror. Finally, I would just pray it away anytime it would begin to surface.

Besides, I had more pressing issues to deal with.

For several months I had experienced pain in my left shoulder. Reluctantly I made an appointment with an orthopedist and had some imaging done. An X-ray didn't show too much, so an MRI was scheduled. Once complete, the radiologists determined I had a torn rotator cuff. My orthopedic surgeon concurred. Since the Christmas holidays were fast approaching, our best option was to wait until the new year to have the surgery and the subsequent long months of physical therapy.

In the weeks that followed, the horrible nightmare returned. Not once but twice. And it became more and more difficult to keep it from creeping into my thoughts during the day as well. Before long I began to equate the trapped feeling from my nightmare with the thoughts of being sedated for surgery. How different would being trapped in a coffin be from being trapped in your own body, conscious but unable to move or communicate with anyone?

Not normally prone to anxiety, I found myself on the edge of panic most of the time. My prayers centered around several verses I had committed to memory. The first, Philippians 4:6, was familiar support—"Be anxious for nothing, but in everything by prayer and supplication, with thanksgiving, let your requests be made known to God" (NKJV). I had used this verse as a personal motto for all the worries that a wife/businesswoman/mother of three encountered daily.

The second passage, Romans 8:38-39, addressed the sense of terror and abandonment that my nightmare had created.

One night I finally broke down and tearfully relayed the story of my nightmare to my husband, Michael. He listened and tried to reassure me, and we prayed together. Thankfully I gained a sense of peace for a few days.

Doubt Creeps In

As the date for surgery grew closer, I continued to pray and tried to guard my mind against slipping back into the memories of my nightmares. I prayed the scriptures again and again. But new thoughts began to plague me. What if there really is no God? What if everything you've learned about Jesus is a lie? What if the Bible isn't true?"

For the first time, I began to doubt the reality of all I'd built my faith on, all of God's promises. Perhaps there is no grand plan for eternity after we die. Perhaps the only existence after death is an eternity of being locked alone in a coffin, without movement, without communication, in darkness and utterly alone.

And despite my prayers and my husband's reassurance that I would be fine, the night before the surgery the nightmare returned, and I was terrified.

The alarm sounded early the next morning as we prepared to go to the hospital. We were on the road just before sunrise. Traffic was light as we made our way through familiar streets. As we approached one major intersection, we were the only vehicle on the road, and I could see ahead a pedestrian on the side of the road. We were less than a block away when he stepped off the curb to cross the intersection, but rather than cross he stopped in the middle of the street and began to walk straight toward our car! I can still remember seeing his face through the windshield as he grew closer and closer.

Rather than try to stop, Michael accelerated and said, "Hold on!" At the very last moment, the man stepped aside, and we drove quickly past him.

I couldn't believe what had just happened. When I asked Michael about not slowing, he said he feared the man was going to carjack our car and that he shouldn't stop. As we continued the trip to the hospital, we even called 911 to let the police know of this man's strange behavior. Just what I needed—more anxiety to add to the day.

A Remarkable Outcome

Within an hour all the necessary pre-op procedures were in process. The medical staff came in to reassure us of the surgical techniques. Two radiologists and two orthopedic surgeons had conferred on the images of the damaged tendons and how best to make the repairs. Michael and I prayed together. I still didn't have answers to the anxious questions that troubled my mind. But sedatives brought a temporary reprieve, and I went off to the operating room.

My next conscious thoughts were of waking up back in my room, fighting the blurred vision and making sense of those moving around me. Noticing the bandages and the equipment in the room. Within just a few minutes, the surgeon returned.

"Good news," he said. "We couldn't find the tear in your rotator cuff. We could only find some minor bone spurs, so we cleaned them up while we were there."

What? No torn muscles and tendons! Even though they were so clearly seen on the MRI images! And just like that, I heard God's voice: "You wondered if I am real? You wondered if I was here with you? I am as close to you as your own left shoulder."

At that moment all the anxiety fell away. The doubt and the confusion about what was real disappeared. The reassurance that God is who He says He is and will do what He says He will do flooded through me again.

"Bless the LORD, O my soul;
And all that is within me, bless His holy name!"

—

PSALM 103:1 (NKJV)

God provided healing for both my shoulder and my soul that morning.

Two days later as I was recuperating at home, Michael brought the morning newspaper to me and asked, "Do you recognize this man?" He showed me a picture, and immediately I saw the same face I had seen through the car windshield the morning we drove to the hospital. The story that followed in the newspaper said that the man carjacked a woman's vehicle later that day and led the police on a high-speed chase before being shot and killed himself.

Even when I wondered, even when I doubted, even amid my panic and anxiety, God never left me! He was always there with me! The words from Romans 8 took on an even deeper meaning.

For I am convinced ... even though I sometimes doubt.

that neither death, nor life ... including sedation or unconsciousness.

nor angels, nor principalities ... including those in this world that would want to harm me.

nor things present, nor things to come ... including all of eternity.

nor powers, nor height, nor depth, nor any other created thing ... including anything I can think, dream or imagine.

will be able to separate us from the love of God that is in Christ Jesus our Lord.

Ginger Moskau Cress is a New Orleans native and retired CPA, having spent most of her career in commercial construction and retail furniture businesses. She has taught Sunday school, small groups and women's Bible studies for more than 40 years. She enjoys reading, baking, traveling, spending time with family and friends, and learning to play the piano. She was married for 36 years until her husband's passing in 2014. In processing her grief, she created the blog WhereIGoFromHere. She is now married to Stephen Cress, and together they enjoy their four children and five grandchildren. Connect with Ginger on Instagram or Facebook.

9

—

Lessons of a Lifetime:

Finding Joy Caring for Parents

By Laurie Cunningham

"I have set the LORD always before me;
because he is at my right hand,
I shall not be shaken.
Therefore my heart is glad,
and my whole being rejoices;
my flesh also dwells secure."

—

PSALM 16:8-9 (ESV)

Aging is a journey we begin the day we are born. For many of us, our parents poured their lives into our lives. They were there for our milestones and joys; they helped us grow into a full life.

They nurtured, nourished and even frustrated us since we were born. Even if you have a distant relationship with your parent(s), you will admit that the parent-child relationship is a profound one that shapes our lives.

I experienced a wonderful and close relationship with my parents. My dad passed away 10 years ago at the age of 84, and my mother will be celebrating her 95th birthday soon! I rejoice in the blessing of having such Christian examples in my life. However, I have learned that longevity is both a blessing and a journey.

The longer we live, the more our relationships with those in our lives change. We are called to care for them in different ways, both physically and emotionally. Over the past several years, I have become keenly aware that caring about someone and caring for someone requires different things from us.

Up until my dad passed away, he lived a very productive and active life. My mother continued to be very independent until four years ago when she suffered a fall. She now lives with limited mobility and growing dependence. This has changed the dynamics with my mother, my siblings and my family.

Because of these changes, I have struggled with the right balance between helping and supporting my mom and taking care of my own family responsibilities. I am so very grateful to still be able to honor my mom, spend time with her, learn from her and share happy times together.

However, caring for my mom requires sacrificial love as well.

Learning to Love in a New Way

Sacrificial love is a hard love. It's not the feel-good, life-is-going-my-way, I-don't-want-any-interruption-to-my-routine kind of love. Sacrificial love calls me to give more of myself and my life than I thought I could. It takes understanding what I can and cannot control ... no matter how worthy my cause may be. It requires yielding to God and His plan for my life and my mother's life.

My mother's journey has been difficult. She prays every day for complete healing. She is sad with the loss of things taken from her in an instant. Dignity, independence and physical strength have been replaced with the challenge of doing simple things that we all take for granted like buttoning a shirt, tying our shoes and basic self-care.

I have sat with her as she reads scripture and prays for spiritual and physical endurance, knowing we both have quietly wondered: Why,

Lord? If I am being honest, experiencing the physical decline of my mom has taken me on a journey of grief, sadness, depression and frustration. I do not want these feelings to make me bitter.

Romans 12:12 instructs us to "Rejoice in hope, be patient in tribulation, be constant in prayer" (ESV). I wish I could say I have always done these things, but often I have acted without joyfulness, patience or prayer.

I want so much for my mom to recover completely that I have overlooked others in this situation. God is calling me to see the bigger picture, not just my perspective.

For example, my siblings are my mother's primary caregivers. They each face their own challenges and need for balance. I must show grace, gentleness and prayerful understanding. I am also learning to give myself grace and accept that I live many states away.

I continue to actively care for my mother, but because my ability to be with her physically is limited, I pray that I can recognize what I can do and willingly take on those responsibilities. I realize we all are working toward filling my mom's life with richness and caring until God calls her home. I know He will bless our efforts if we seek His will in this process.

For those of you who might be traveling a similar journey, I'd like to share several lessons I've taken from this chapter of my life:

- Admit you don't have all the answers. Learn to be kind to yourself. Be honest and truthful with how you are feeling.
- Realize you are not in control but that you can control certain things. Seek God's guidance to identify what you can and should be doing. Make an impact in areas where you are able.
- Live in community. Confiding in and talking to people you trust is so important. Without that, you see things only from your own vantage point. Share your experiences with others and seek godly advice from them. Let someone help you carry your burdens.
- Remember that this situation will change. Be flexible and try fresh solutions.

- Collaborate where you can, and value the contribution each person makes, even if you may at times be called to give more of yourself and your life than others.

Finally, God is teaching me how to live with the mindset of joy ... no matter the circumstances. Joy comes from honoring, trusting in and seeking God in every part of life.

As He revealed to me in Psalm 16, verses 8-9: He is always before me. He is at my right hand, and I will not be shaken. My heart is glad, and my whole being rejoices. In His love, I am secure.

Laurie Cunningham is a true Gulf Coast girl, born in Mobile, Alabama, and raised in Gulfport, Mississippi. She is happiest on summer days spent with family and friends. Laurie attended the University of New Orleans where she obtained a BA in drama and communications. Her career path included television production, corporate sales and music education. Currently, she operates a gift boutique where she enjoys getting to know her customers and sharing her appreciation for handcrafted and vintage items. She has been married to Bob for 25 years, and they have two daughters, Ava and Audrey. Her family has lived in many locations throughout the U.S. but currently resides near Raleigh, North Carolina.

10

His Faithful Feathers:
From Cowered in Ruin
to Covered in Righteousness
By Jennifer Elwood

> *"He will cover you with his feathers,*
> *and under his wings you will find refuge;*
> *his faithfulness will be your shield and rampart."*
>
> —
>
> **PSALM 91:4 (NIV)**

On my way up, I never felt so low. The airplane carrying us paid no attention to my heavy soul as lift forces took us toward a cruising altitude of 30,000 feet. Hot tears spilled as I strived to hold myself together.

A few weeks before, I'd returned home to London with my toddler-aged son from an international family visit. Upon arrival, my then-husband slammed my jet-lagged mind with the news I never thought I would hear: he wanted a divorce. Devastated, I fought through disjointed circadian rhythms to deal with the mess of packing everything up and returning to the U.S.

I felt so utterly alone.

When we finally boarded the plane to make our way back to

Washington State, I consoled myself with thoughts of access to a child cot. When booking the flight, I snagged a front seat and imagined several hours with an empty lap, my son and I peacefully asleep. But my lanky toddler was too tall, and I faced *nine* hours in a middle seat with a boy in my lap. I rapidly punched the call button and asked to change seats, but the flight was full. Panic set in.

A desperate *HELP ME* prayer flew to Heaven as I spied two seats together across the aisle.

When the doors finally closed, I leaped from my seat. With complete desperation, I asked the young man on the aisle if we could *please move* into those two seats. Unfazed by my harried request, he kindly acquiesced and offered to swap. All three seats would be ours.

I gratefully accepted with bewilderment. Who trades an aisle seat with extra room for a crummy middle seat? Well … he did. After my grateful tears dried up, we stretched out and rested. Refuge appeared in those seats: a gift from the Lord.

I've pondered this event that occurred back in 2006 many times. And I must confess, I was puzzled for years over one particular detail—why *three* seats? The extravagance of extra space poked around my thoughts until one day the answer flew into my mind: Jesus Himself was in that extra seat.

Who leaves the perfection of Heaven to be with an emotional wreck on a plane? Well … He did! When I consider the event in hindsight, I'm overwhelmed by a tranquil scene. Jesus occupied the seat on the aisle—with arms appearing as shimmering wings—encircled in a tight embrace around two hurting souls. They headed toward the unknown but, at that moment, everything felt right because the Lord sheltered us in His perfect protection.

Little did I know, that event was preparing me for lift-off in my faith journey. As I grew in belief, Jesus began to send physical feathers to gain my attention when fear threatened to overtake me. So now, I tangibly experience what became my life verse: "He will cover you with his feathers, and under his wings you will find refuge; his faithfulness will be your shield and rampart" (Psalm 91:4 NIV).

Sparked by the persistent feathers sent from my faithful God, I've studied this verse inside and out. So put the seat back up and the tray tables in locked position, because what I have to share landed my faith on solid ground.

The first part of this verse impressed me to study feathers, and what I learned astounds me. When holding up a single feather, it appears soft and delicate. But viewed under a microscope, each individual strand contains thousands of razor-like protrusions that bind the material together. So when magnified, a feather dons the appearance of barbed wire. And when feathers layer atop one another, it creates a nearly impenetrable barrier.

To me, it's a beautiful metaphor for our Savior. When I consider Jesus newly born, He appears soft and tender. When I think of Jesus, battle-worn and adorned with thorns on the way to the cross, I see the binding under the microscope. He embodies delicate and fierce as He provides perfect refuge.

In the latter half of this verse, "shield" and "rampart" are likened to God's faithfulness. And I adore the picture I now have in mind since studying these weapons of war. The word used to describe this particular shield is specific; thick and protective, it covers a warrior from head to toe. When placed next to each other, they protect an entire battle line. This detail taught me that God's faithful refuge isn't partial. The space under His wings provides full coverage.

As I looked at the word for rampart more closely, I discovered the translations using "buckler" are more accurate. This is a small, round, wooden shield worn on the forearm. My favorite feature is that it's used for both defense and offense.

I've learned that God's glorious faithfulness appears as a war-ravaged shield that not only protects but simultaneously fights against the evil that threatens me.

My life will never be unblemished—I've lived through many trials and will continue to. But I've landed my faith on the promise of God's faithfulness. I praise God that His soft yet fierce protection offers me peace in the midst of trials. There's no place I'd rather be; tucked under the safety of His wings, on the lookout for feathers floating down, reminding me of His perfect refuge.

Jennifer Elwood hosts the Refuge Podcast and Bible Study Community where women cultivate their faith in the shelter of God's Word. Jennifer is a Yakima, Washington resident, lover of Jesus, wife of Tom, mom of three and bonus mom and grandma. She's a travel fanatic and a coffee addict, and she enjoys nerding out on biblical context when studying the Bible. Going to Israel for the first time in 2015 sparked her desire to write, and she has not stopped since. She's the author of Counting Up to Christmas: Twenty-Four Gifts from the Gospel of Luke and Counting Up to Christmas: The Companion Cookbook.

11

My Way, the Highway or God's Way

By Jana MacCarrie Fraley

"A man's heart plans his way, but the LORD directs his steps."

—

PROVERBS 16:9 (NKJV)

I grew up the only daughter of a ranchman who was strict with my brothers and me, yet still loved us in his own way. He taught us the importance of hard work and honesty but only occasionally shared words of encouragement or love. Mom balanced Dad's toughness with tender wisdom. She took every opportunity to share her deep faith in the Lord and life lessons as we lived, worked and played together on the ranch.

It was a wonderful childhood that allowed my imagination to thrive; I was a head-in-the-clouds dreamer and an avid reader. If I wasn't reading, I loved making up stories in my head while I was on horseback following a string of cattle, fixing a fence in a pasture or on a piece of equipment in the hayfield.

My favorite story to write was my own.

I didn't necessarily have "high" expectations, but I did have very *specific* expectations, dreams and plans. I wasn't afraid to "tell" God how well I had mapped my life out! Of course, I'd also share those dreams with my mom while we did chores, rode horseback or worked in the kitchen together.

I was going to marry Georgie, the ranch boy down the road. We'd have six kids, all of whom would have names that began with the letter "K." We'd live in a single-wide trailer house within a few feet of the old ranch house I grew up in—our front door facing their back door—and we'd all be together on the ranch, living happily ever after!

As the years went by, I had to give up on bits and pieces of that beautiful, well-thought-out plan, but parts of it remained. I had to let go of the dream of marrying Georgie because he never saw me as anything more than his little sister's annoying friend. My dream house changed from a trailer house to an old ranch house of my own. And my mom convinced me that living next door to them wouldn't be as fun as I thought!

Yet, my life-mapping tendencies were still the same as when I was a little girl; they just became more realistic. I eventually met and married a ranch boy, but instead of living down the road, he was from across the state. My husband shared my dream of having children, just not six! We settled on having two, and I believed I could convince him to have a third in due time.

In those early days of marriage, I would spend my morning "quiet time" sharing my hopes and dreams for the future with God. I wasn't praying as much as I was telling Him how I thought my future should pan out: Someday, we'd return to one of our family's ranches and spend our life raising cattle and kids. We'd begin our family within two years, and two years later we'd welcome baby number two. Twins would be great, so I wouldn't have to convince my husband of that third baby.

I thought I was trusting God, but my mom would often paraphrase The Living Bible: "We should make plans, but we need to count on God to direct us." And I did count on and trust Him … just as long as He was willing to do things my way!

My plans eventually took a detour, and God began to shape and mold my faith in Him and not in my dreams. Instead of another baby coming two years later, it would take 11 years to get pregnant again because of health issues. Getting back to ranching took even longer. Being on my family's ranch and living close to my parents would never happen. All my well-made plans and expectations slowly began to unravel.

Disappointment defined my life. And comparison was my worst enemy.

Even when our hopes were realized and we had our son, I was still eaten up with jealousy toward friends who were raising their children on family ranches. I missed the lifestyle, and I missed being close to my parents.

And then, when I was in my mid-40s, we lost my mom in a horse accident on the ranch. The resulting grief meant I faced the most significant defeat and disappointment of my dreams. I would never experience raising my kids on the family ranch with her guidance nearby. My children would no longer experience the wisdom their grandmother poured into their lives.

I became angry at God because He wasn't answering my prayers the way I thought He should. As a result, my dreams for my future were replaced with fear, discouragement and even dread.

I struggle with the need to have control of my life. I often fight a my-way-or-the-highway sort of attitude. I have often felt that if I could control my life and the events surrounding me, I would experience security and contentment. I believed God would see my plans were good plans, and He'd bless them. However, when I began to see that this wasn't always the case, I encountered doubt and despair.

But God, in His unending grace and mercy, knew that my tendency to control would cause many heartaches, wounded relationships and devastating disappointments.

When I look back, I recognize this is where He began a refining work in my life, using the heat of my disappointed plans and burning away the dross of my need for control. He brought me to a crossroads where I had to choose His will or my way. What resulted is a purified faith that recognizes the grander perspective of God's sovereignty and intentions in all areas of my life.

Making plans is not a bad thing in and of itself; God created us to think, plan and dream. The problem arises when our dreams become more about having things turn out our way than trusting in His good plan for our lives. The truth is that we aren't the lord of our lives—He is! It's the Lord who directs our steps and guides our lives. Therefore, every plan we make should be held with open hands and in humility, willingly releasing those plans to Him and surrendering to His ultimate will for our lives.

Ultimately, God's plans are always much better than those we devise on our own. Of course, we can make plans according to our heart's desires, but when we trust God to lead us, we can know that our steps will not be outside the government of God.

It's not that any of my plans were "bad" plans, it's just that God determines what will occur in my life, and He is abundantly able to do more than I can ask or imagine (Ephesians 3:20). No matter how "good" my plans are, His plans are always better. Over the years, I've learned it's not "my way or the highway" that I really want, but always God's way!

Jana MacCarrie Fraley is a Christian writer, speaker, ranch wife and mom. Her passion is discipling and encouraging women as they pursue faith in Jesus by seeking God's truth, developing a biblical worldview and finding contentment. She has collaborated on Tapestry of Grace and written The Truth Journal: A 30-Day Guided Journal to Combat the Lies of the Enemy With the Truth of God's Word. Jana has written for Kindred Mom, Living By Design Ministries, The Joyful

Life Magazine, Brave Women Series, Heartbreak to Strength Blog, and Faith Storytellers. She writes from her Wyoming ranch where she, her husband Mike, and two children, Hannah and Kade, have made a life together raising cattle.

12

How To Trust the Promise-Keeper from the Slice of Earth Beneath Your Feet

By Twyla Franz

"You keep every promise you've ever made to me!
Since your love for me is constant and endless,
I ask you, Lord, to finish every good thing
that you've begun in me!"

—

PSALM 138:8 (TPT)

When your cell phone rings with the news that makes an original, *life-is-going-to-be-beautiful-and-also-hard-and-different* diagnosis sound breezy, your heart lodges itself in the pit of your stomach. You scratch notes on a paper towel as you lean against the kitchen counter. Adding "funeral plans" to the list makes you fall apart inside. How desperately you wish there was threadbare hope for this dear, beautiful soul …

The crater carved in an instant creates the capacity to trust. So you read Psalm 139 aloud into the phone in your bravest voice because you know it's as true today as it's ever been.

The next morning, you put your two hands on your paper towel notes, insert a name, and pray Psalm 139 again. Declare that even now God is holy and worthy and the Author of the best plans. Because though your heart is broken, God's promises are not.

Your gaze turns to the verse right before Psalm 139. It's marked in multiple colors, evidence you've anchored yourself here for weeks. You trace the lines with your finger as you read: "You keep every promise you've ever made to me! Since your love for me is constant and endless, I ask you, Lord, to finish every good thing that you've begun in me!" (Psalm 138:8 TPT)

You whisper these words when the weight of a task you cannot accomplish on your own pulls you to face-down surrender. The plumb line through the worship songs you play loud in your Beats and pen into Bible margins. They've spurred an insistent and insatiable desire to seek God. To linger longer. Long for His touch. His face. His relentless grace and wide-open love.

You're typically not one to cry, but lately, you've been living on the raw edge of tears, where the space between Heaven and right here feels especially thin. And now the tears break hot and heavy, splattering the note-filled paper towel.

> God is Promise-Keeper.
> Creator of only good things—*gifts*.
> The Finisher of Everything He Begins.
> El Roi. The God Who Sees.
> Shepherd and Very Best Friend.
> Heart Examiner.
> Blessing Imparter.
> Masterpiece Creator.
> Light Bringer.
> The Everywhere God who hears, knows, cares and groans—
> because His heart breaks too.

He makes us all "mysteriously complex"—even those He calls home early—and *everything* He does is "marvelously breathtaking" (Psalm

139:14 TPT). It's He who "formed every bone," "carefully, skillfully [shaping her] from nothing to something" (v. 15). Who "saw who [He] created [her] to be before," before the details of her one precious life were known (v. 16). In this, in *all* of this, His gracious "hand of love" is ever "upon [her] life" (v. 5).

Your eyes find a verse you've quoted often, and you choke a little as you pray through it:

"Every single moment you are thinking of me! [*Of her!*] How precious and wonderful to consider that you cherish [her] constantly in your every thought." (v. 17)

Right there at the edge of the counter, bent over that list on a paper towel, you thank God for these promises with what you call "nevertheless gratitude." The thanksgiving that comes *before* the breakthrough, the answer, the shift, the restoration. Because God is *good* regardless of which side of Heaven the healing comes from.

Maybe it's this nevertheless lesson that's best prepared you for the things that break you wide open. You know in your soul that God never changes. That you can boldly trust Him. That He's good and faithful, holy and true. And you've got direct access to Him, even when His answer is hard to understand from the slice of earth beneath your feet.

King David grappled with the word "nevertheless" in the book of Psalms, and here's where he landed: gratitude is a before, not an after, *because gratitude teaches our hearts to trust the good hand of our heavenly Father*. In Psalm 89:52, David pivots from complaint to praise. His circumstances hadn't changed—yet. So he praised God because He changes *never*. And this bold, even-now declaration unlocked adoration and worship. Cleared his lens. Righted his heart.

Devote a life to learning the character of God as David did, and you'll trust the faithfulness and goodness of God even when your mind lags behind. You'll name what you know to be true on those days tense with question marks and ampersands. And thanks, you'll discover, builds a bridge from the ache of right now to the hope of not yet.

God literally CANNOT break His own promises. Back down on what He's said. Reduce his "endless and constant" love for her or me or you.

No matter how raw your right now feels, may this love find you. Melt your clenched fists. Unlock awe and spontaneous praise. Build a hope bridge from your pain to One who knows you, holds you and heals you.

Maybe your new way forward looks like nevertheless gratitude. Praising to the Promise-Keeper who never begins what He doesn't intend to finish. Who holds the bridge, the ground on both sides, the air above and the water beneath. Who's bigger than we could ever see from standing in one spot.

Twyla Franz is a growing voice in the missional living niche whose words appear in publications like Relevant and Her View From Home. She founded The Uncommon Normal in 2019 to uncomplicate missional neighboring, help others get to know their neighbors and inspire faith that has a ripple effect. Twyla has an e-guide, Pinterest for Writers: How to Explode Your Growth with the Tools You Already Have, and a book, Cultivating a Missional Life: A 30-Day Devotional to Gently Help You Open Your Heart, Home, and Life to Your Neighbors. Twyla and her family live in Lexington, Kentucky, where they host a neighborhood missional community.

13

A Different Perspective:

Mental Illness Made Me a Better Person

By Darcie Fuqua

> *"To all who mourn in Israel,*
> *he will give a crown of beauty for ashes,*
> *a joyous blessing instead of mourning,*
> *festive praise instead of despair.*
> *In their righteousness,*
> *they will be like great oaks*
> *that the LORD has planted*
> *for his own glory."*
>
> —
>
> **ISAIAH 61:3 (NLT)**

"This wasn't the plan, God. Remember, we made a deal."

Looking back over my life, I recall God-breathed seasons of blessings where things looked far better than anything I could imagine. But I also consider the past months, even years, and ruminate on the fact that things don't always turn out like I expect—not even remotely. I've lived the highs and lows of this rollercoaster ride and muddled through the mundane. And somewhere over the last eight years, I've slowly learned to relinquish control and surrender to the One who holds it all. Because "Many are the plans in a person's heart, but it is the LORD's purpose that prevails" Proverbs 19:21 (NIV).

The Metamorphosis

On one scorching, sticky day in the middle of August, I plopped onto the back porch bench, seeking refuge under the humming fans. The sun-faded pillows and worn-out wicker created a sacred place where I went to meet with Jesus. And the cushion became threadbare in this tumultuous season I had been experiencing with my health.

As days lingered on but somehow steadily marched forward, my prayers began to change course. The lamenting and pity-party conversations turned to questions of transformation: "How, Lord, will you use this trial for your glory?" When all I saw was a damaged body with a defective brain, Christ dared me to see it as a gift.

That's when I saw a stunning gift! It was attached to the bottom of the table right by my bench, only noticed when you lie down. Through a lowered and blurry gaze, I saw a green chrysalis with its beautiful crown of gold transforming right before my eyes. It was a physical representation of the extraordinary work our God can do within the confines of dark spaces.

Every morning, I peeked out the back door to witness the changes of the caterpillar, petitioning the Lord to make sure I didn't miss the moment the butterfly emerged and flew away. To my dismay, I saw the empty cocoon one morning and feared I had missed the monarch butterfly's arrival. But there she was, hanging on the leg of the table. Not quite ready to flap her wings precisely, unsure of the right way to fly. The monarch trained her wings slowly as she adjusted to the light.

And then she took flight! I watched her brilliant orange-and-black wings fly over my fence into the azul-colored sky until she was far out of sight. I marveled that she was once a caterpillar restrained to crawling around, then temporarily imprisoned in a cocoon, and now had wings. And with those wings came a completely different perspective of her surroundings.

I wondered if God could do the same thing with me and give me a different outlook on my trials. *Would He ever turn my ashes into a crown of gold?*

My Cocoon Story

Eight years ago, two months after the arrival of my first beautiful baby boy, my life took a drastic turn in the blink of an eye. I experienced a rapid onset of postpartum psychosis (my initial diagnosis). Since then, I've experienced three more rapid onsets of catatonia. Despite consistent medication, I had an episode after five years of remission. Catatonia is a rare psychomotor disease studied for over 150 years, and experts still don't know exactly why it happens.

Each time I have a catatonic episode, I am hospitalized. It always happens on a Thursday evening, and I wake up like normal on a Saturday morning—the strangest anomaly no doctor can explain. Sometimes I remember everything, and other times I think I'm asleep for a 24-hour span.

But I always remember the precious souls I meet during my hospital stays.

Since I am no longer a mental hospital rookie, I try to learn God's lessons within the confines of four walls. I've learned to ask the Holy Spirit, "What can I gain from being here?" I try to lean into the whispers of the Spirit to hear the answer to "Who do you want me to speak with this time?"

I've sat with veterans from each military branch and earnestly soaked in their stories. One was a gorgeous college girl who battled anorexia. Another time I walked the halls with a man who was physically and mentally abused as a child. In front of the only sunlit window in the hall, I conversed with a beautiful lady who survived being shot 21 times.

There have been many prayers with women who have a long history of sexual abuse. I've played card games with the shaky hands of men and women detoxing off of street drugs. And once a prostitute held my hands and assured me that God would restore everything I had lost. She was right.

These are only a few of the people who have changed my life, humbled me and tugged at my heartstrings. Despite their detrimental circumstances, most men and women showed unwavering faith in our unseen God. Over the last eight years, God has shown me several times how easy it is to take for granted the creature comforts I am blessed with. He has shown me the pits of affliction and oppression that the poor in Spirit endure.

And it has made me a better person.

I'd love to say that I emerge from my dark cocoon ready to take flight each time, but I have a mourning period where I deal with depression, anger, resentment and fear of what the future may hold with my unpredictable disease. I have long conversations with God on the same bench that now has sun-bleached, frayed wicker. God gently reminds me that He woke me up again and saved my life. He pushes me to see unpredictable life events as a gift—His story to be told. He tells me parts of the beautiful love story He hasn't finished writing, and I hang onto His promises with a white-knuckled grip.

And He reminds me to look all around me. He is not as unseen as some believe. The Holy Spirit gave me eyes and ears to witness God's miraculous works surrounding me. He reminds me to keep my eyes straight ahead toward the Promised Land. And if I am to look back, look back and search for Him because I will always find evidence of His presence.

I often find myself looking in the rearview mirror to catch a glimpse of my two precious, healthy boys. And I think to myself that I would do it all again—every last bit of the past eight years—to have those boys in my life.

I imagine that's the same thing Jesus thinks when He looks at you and me. He says, "Lovely one, I'd do it all again just to have you."

Darcie Fuqua is a business analyst, Auburn grad (War Eagle!), Christian blogger, podcast host and mental health advocate. She is from the deep south of Alabama, where she currently resides with her husband, two energetic, fun-loving boys and a dog named Charlie. She loves sinking her toes in the sand, cuddling with her boys and having great conversations over a table of good food. You can read more of her writing on her website, www.leightonlane.com, and connect with her on Facebook and Instagram. Check out Darcie's latest project as cohost of the podcast Therapy in 10.

14

When God Says His Grace is Enough:

Learning to Abide Within the Limits God Allows

By Renée Gotcher

> *"And He said to me,*
> *'My grace is sufficient for you,*
> *for My strength is made*
> *perfect in weakness.'"*
>
> —
>
> **2 CORINTHIANS 12:9 (NKJV)**

The bright fluorescent lights illuminating the cold, cluttered hospital room felt like a penetrating spotlight scrutinizing my bewildered state. As I lay there alone on the crisply papered bed in a tangle of beeping machines—awaiting test results and praying for an actionable diagnosis—my thoughts raced in search of rational answers.

It was my second trip to the emergency room in a short span of three days. And until those two suburban-peace-shattering ambulance rides, I'd never been to the ER as a patient. In my trauma-free, relatively healthy 39 years of life, my hospital visits included bringing babies into the world, taking an injured child in for stitches, and meeting my husband after a mountain-biking accident—all perfectly ordinary reasons a married mother with an active family might find herself there.

Yet here I was—again—with symptoms that didn't have a tidy explanation. Unfortunately, I would soon learn that the standard battery of tests following my admittance didn't shed any light on the situation. As if she thought her words would ease my concerns, the ER doctor calmly and matter-of-factly explained that all the tests had come back normal, and panic attacks were her best explanation for my symptoms.

Panic attacks? How could the suffocating discomfort in my throat, tightening chest, racing heartbeat, tingling waves of nerve pain and constant nausea be caused by anxiety that I was apparently unaware of, revealing itself now in the form of panic attacks? It didn't seem possible that simple emotions such as stress or anxiety could lead to symptoms so unsettling that I would feel compelled to dial 911 for a second time that week. After all, I was a self-sufficient, business-owning, blogging, homeschooling mother of three who never let a ball drop, even though my husband regularly traveled for work and I managed the household on my own much of the time. I was *not* an anxious person—in fact, I was known for my ability to handle stress well. I sat in stunned silence, then immediately resolved to find a *real* cause for my body's distress by getting a second opinion.

Six months later, I came to accept that these ER visits were just the beginning of a decade-long battle with generalized anxiety that eventually required medication to manage and counseling to understand. What I assumed would be a stopgap measure to return stability to my body chemistry turned into years on medication. All the while, I continued to pray for complete recovery, feeling confident that God would lead me to a medication-free finish line as I sought alternative solutions that might provide long-term healing. After all, why would God allow the anxiety coursing through my body to persist, limiting my ability to perform at full capacity? Wouldn't an inspiring testimony of mental health victory be powerful—and preferable—as a ministry tool for an anxiety-ridden culture?

In 2 Corinthians 12:8, the apostle Paul expresses a similar sentiment: "Concerning this thing [a thorn in the flesh], I pleaded with the Lord three times that it might depart from me" (NKJV).

I can relate to Paul's persistence. It was a reasonable request for a faithful apostle consumed with fulfilling his role in the great commission. He was going about the Lord's work every minute of every day, under constant threat of physical persecution (which he endured many times). Why wouldn't he ask the Lord to be relieved of this hindrance? It seemed like the obvious solution.

Yet despite all that Paul wanted to accomplish for his Savior, he was not only "given" a thorn in the flesh (v. 7), he was also presented with a different remedy entirely: God's sustaining grace. "And He said to me, 'My grace is sufficient for you...'" the apostle reported (12:9).

I'll be the first to admit that I was uncomfortable with God's response to Paul, especially when it seemed clear that He had the same message for me. As much as I wanted complete healing and lasting relief from physical anxiety symptoms, God offered me daily grace instead.

God's grace took many forms: a faith-reinforcing scripture image popping up on my Instagram feed when I really needed those living words; a spot-on devotional addressing the very concerns that had consumed my waking thoughts that morning; an acquaintance reaching out unexpectedly to meet an unspoken need, or a friend offering to keep me accountable to daily nature walks that would provide short bursts of physical and emotional relief. On the most difficult days, when anxiety symptoms were so unpredictable that I feared I would fail to complete minimal work and family duties, God's grace provided just enough sure footing for me to reach the evening hours, when I could safely retreat into my room and collapse on my bed.

Maybe you've been pleading with the Lord to remove a "thorn" in your life. And you're struggling to understand why God would allow it when you could be so much more productive and effective without this painful impediment holding you back. Maybe you've even experienced or witnessed miraculous provision and divine healing in the past, and now you wrestle with the notion that God might not intervene before you break into a thousand pieces. I know what it feels like to desperately hope that God's response to your prayers will not be the same as His answer to Paul.

However, I now have a deeper understanding of Paul's confident conclusion on the matter: "For when I am weak, then I am strong" (2 Corinthians 12:10). I know what it feels like to be sustained by God's grace alone, providing what I need to get from one moment to the next, one day at a time. I've learned to stop looking for pain-free shortcuts to the perceived finish line of my problems. That perspective feeds my self-sufficiency, but God's Word instructs me to surrender that control and rest in His provision, His daily grace.

I recently had another opportunity to get reacquainted with God's daily grace. In the fall of 2022, after being medication-free for 18 months, I found myself back in another doctor's office, awaiting test results to see whether resurfacing anxiety symptoms could possibly have some other cause. And I prayed once again for God to take these symptoms away without medication. Why wouldn't I?

However, this time I also prayed, "Not my will, but Your will be done, Father. I trust You to complete the good work that You began in me, and I know that no physical ailment can prevent me from accomplishing the purposes You have for me."

I have learned to pray for what I need *today*, be thankful for what God's grace provides for me *today*, and trust that He will do the same thing again tomorrow. It's my prayer that whatever "thorn" you are praying to be removed, or whatever state of brokenness is making you feel incapable of serving God to your fullest potential, you would grab hold of the all-sufficient grace your Heavenly Father is offering you *today*. He invites you to come to Him every morning, surrendering both your worst anxieties and best-laid plans, and rest in His provision of daily grace and strength. Because when you are weak, He is strong!

Renée Gotcher is a writer, editor and editorial consultant with nearly three decades of experience in the print and online publishing world. She is a wife of 28 years, a homeschooling mother of three daughters (two now in college) and an outdoor-loving Colorado transplant. Renée began her editorial career in journalism, working her way to the position of executive editor for a national technology magazine. Renée currently draws on her years of editorial experience to partner with emerging Christian writers and help them turn their stories into compelling content with eternal impact. She also shares her journey to relieve anxiety, restore peace, and revive hope by stepping outside for sacred walks with her Savior on Instagram (@thepaceofgrace_reneegotcher) and her blog (reneegotcher.com). Connect with Renée on her website, Instagram or Facebook.

15

The Good, Unusual Lessons of Painful Trials:

A Pathway to Growth

By Pamela Henkelman

"But he knows where I am going.
And when he tests me,
I will come out as pure as gold."

—

JOB 23:10 (NLT)

Have you ever been through a season of life that was meant to destroy you, but God brought immeasurable growth and strength to your soul? Let me tell you about my season of refining.

The Refining Fire

I was on the highway again, taking the one-hour drive to St. Paul, Minnesota, so I could be with my young husband for another week's stay at the Multiple Sclerosis Center at Fairview Riverside Hospital. There he was pumped full of steroids to tame the inflammation that attacked his nerves, leaving him with a new tremor, spasm or disability. Chronic progressive MS was a beast that could not be tamed. The disease had upended our family in profound ways.

A 90s song was playing on Christian radio, including these lyrics: "Life is hard, but God is good." The contrast of this statement pierced my soul. As I drove, I acknowledged this trial was very difficult.

My heart broke because of my husband's disability. My young, strong spouse was gone. Everything in our lives had changed. Our days revolved around endless hospitalizations, coupled with managing increasing disability. The bad news kept piling up. Physical, emotional and financial loss enveloped us.

We were stretched and humbled by this trial, yet my husband and I sensed God's presence. We felt His love. How could it be? Listening to this song opened a floodgate of tears as I cried for an hour, all the way to the hospital. Tears provided the release I needed from the stress, while I simultaneously whispered thanks to God for sustaining us through these dark months.

Those two-and-a-half years of struggle were fertile ground where God planted my roots deep in Him. He taught me to trust when my world completely fell apart. When my husband's physical state only got worse and the doctor recommended placing him in a nursing home, it was preparation for every trial I would face in the future.

In the crushing, I learned to rely on God, and I walked in His presence each day. It hurt, yet I felt completely held, safe and secure. I poured over His Word where He spoke promises of presence, safety, peace and provision. I never felt abandoned or forsaken. I was called to fully trust Him.

Though outwardly everything was falling apart, inwardly I felt resolved and confident that one day our God would rescue us from all this pain.

Then, two-and-a-half years after the trial began, God ended it at a church service when my husband experienced miraculous healing. He shuffled into the service completely disabled, taking 17 daily prescriptions, and left the service chasing our two-year-old toddler, his body completely restored. We serve a miracle-working God!

As glorious as the miracle was, we didn't forget the lessons learned in the crushing. God refined us in profound ways. This is the good He brings from our troubles.

We're familiar with the story of Job, who experienced immense loss: financial, physical and relational. He lost his wealth, his family and his physical strength as his life was plunged into suffering. His wife and friends abandoned him, but He held on to God. In Job 23:10, we see his trust in God and his understanding that through the refining process, he would be made stronger: "But he knows where I am going. And when he tests me, I will come out as pure as gold."

Yes, we bristle when trials come. We beg God to rescue us, and often bitterness forms in our souls when we feel abandoned by God. But what could our lives look like if we approached our trials from a heart of submission, anchored in grace and absolute trust in God?

Four Things You Can Learn from Trials

1. Trials will come.

You're often surprised when hardship comes your way because you spend most of your days dodging trouble. You long for comfort. Yet this passage clearly says when troubles of any kind come your way. Not if, but when. God acknowledges they will come. Instead of being surprised, you can accept God's hand, knowing full well He has a purpose in trials. They are to refine, mature and grow your relationship with God. They force you to draw near to God to receive His strength, and that might be the greatest gift of all.

> *"Dear brothers and sisters,*
> *when troubles of any kind come your way,*
> *consider it an opportunity for great joy.*
> *For you know that when your faith is tested,*
> *your endurance has a chance to grow."*
> —
> **JAMES 1:2-3 (NLT)**

2. You are promised God's presence.

You often assume the Lord has left you when trouble comes, but nowhere does scripture say that. In fact, the Word is filled with promises of God's nearness. There is never a moment when you are without God. You cannot escape His presence. You will find Him when you read His Word, have honest conversations with Him through prayer, and have faith in Him. Understanding that God is near you will help you run to Him for reassurance and strength. You'll be buoyed by your connection with God.

"God is our refuge and strength,
always ready to help in times of trouble."
—
PSALM 46:1 (NLT)

3. Your attitude matters.

Grumbling and complaining are the surest way to invite despair and hopelessness into your journey. It's normal to be afraid and upset when your life falls apart, but your attitude will impact how you move through the trial. Instead of railing at God, adopt a posture of gratitude and quiet trust. Humbly submit your heart to God and ask Him to teach you His ways. The peace you desire is carried on the wings of a heart that trusts God.

"Blessed is the man who trusts in the LORD,
whose trust is the LORD."
—
JEREMIAH 17:7 (ESV)

4. You will be changed.

Just as fire refines and purifies metal, a trial will polish your character. When you allow God to be your partner, trials build you and change you into a vessel He can use. He'll refine the rough edges of your character and soften your calloused heart. This beautiful transformation will be a testimony for all to see as you shine God's light through the way you live.

"We can rejoice, too, when we run into problems and trials,
for we know that they help us develop endurance.
And endurance develops strength of character,
and character strengthens our confident hope of salvation."
—
ROMANS 5:3-4 (NLT)

No one wants to go through troubles, yet God does some of His best work in our impossible situations. When trials come, and He promised that they would, we have an opportunity to build a deeper bond with God as we allow Him to shape and form our hearts. Then, as we simply trust Him and rely on Him, He will bring redemption from our adversities.

Pamela Henkelman is a life coach for midlife moms, speaker, writer and host of The Midlife Momma Podcast. She is passionate about encouraging women, particularly the often-forgotten group of moms with adult children. Pamela helps these moms navigate their changing roles and build stronger relationships with their grown children. As a mom of five kids and two grandsons, Pamela has firsthand experience with the challenges and joys of navigating the empty nest phase of life. She and her husband, who is a pastor, are living their best empty-nest life and loving every minute of it. Connect with her on Facebook, Instagram, her website or The Midlife Momma Podcast.

16

Finding and Embracing God's Plan in Uncertain Times:

Lessons from the Pandemic

By Heather Jeffery

*"Now to him who is able to do immeasurably
more than all we ask or imagine,
according to his power that is at work within us,
to him be glory in the church
and in Christ Jesus throughout all generations,
for ever and ever! Amen."*

—

EPHESIANS 3:20-21 (NIV)

Covid-19 was something unheard of until it became the primary topic of all news channels. I was already carrying a heavy burden at that time. My marriage had been unraveling for years and was barely hanging on by a tattered thread. As a working mom, I prayed for God to open a door for more time at home as things were in desperate need of repair. I specifically asked for a slower pace to breathe fresh life into my family.

God is capable of working all things for good, so a pandemic would surely be no exception. Although the circumstances were not what I envisioned, the world paused, and a pause was what I needed. However, my world in healthcare had no pause.

I was the rehabilitation director in an assisted living community, which rapidly went into lockdown with a strict no-visitor policy. The demands to meet the physical and emotional needs of residents were overwhelming. While the rest of the nation documented their new homeschooling routine with walks in the park and family meals on social media, I left my children home to navigate online school alone while my husband and I went to work as "essential workers," a new term we adopted during the pandemic.

Time went on, and my children adapted to virtual life with minimal adult presence. However, new worries surfaced. They were already facing our impending divorce, and now they were socially isolated with strict orders to stay inside for safety.

It all seemed so unfair. Did God not see what my family was going through? Had he not heard my prayers? I watched as friends and family posted all their "togetherness" on social media with post after post about enjoying the slower pace. *This was MY prayer, Lord. Why are you giving it to everyone but me?* It would take a few months for the entitlement mindset to transform into a heart of gratitude (but spoiler alert: I eventually got there).

Although the world was experiencing the pandemic together, we were all living very different realities. While I longed to be home caring for my family, others desperately prayed for work as finances dwindled.

My days were long, but time with God was non-negotiable. I had been navigating the turbulent waters of a destructive marriage for several years, and God was the source of every ounce of strength I mustered. It was not only revitalizing to drink from His Word each day, it was necessary for me to function.

I grew close to one particular resident during this season. Mrs. Pearl's husband had a progressive disease that was slowly stealing his mind and his mobility. Her sweet, loving husband was becoming more confused with less of his personality present each day. I too was watching someone I loved fade away as my life partner morphed into someone I no longer recognized.

With each conversation, I realized how similar our very different situations were. Although Mrs. Pearl's husband had been a tender and caring leader through 70 years of marriage, she was also facing decisions on her own. We were not that different, after all.

Although my days were long and burdensome, I always made time for Mrs. Pearl. I was still processing my own freshly inflicted emotional wounds, requiring me to pause as I silently prayed by her door before entering. *God, I don't know what I have to offer as I am mentally and physically exhausted, but YOU are my strength. Fill me with your wisdom and words to minister truth to another hurting heart.*

We were both grieving the unexpected loss of someone who was very much still alive. This type of grief is complicated and not readily accepted. Well-meaning phrases such as, "At least your husband is still alive," fail to provide comfort; words such as these add a layer of guilt and shame as very real feelings are invalidated.

Death is definitely painful, but the process of grieving the deceased comes with some level of closure that simply does not exist when grieving the loss of one still living.

Each day Mrs. Pearl and I worked through her latest challenges to establish self-care strategies, truth-in-love responses and necessary boundaries. We discussed when it was safe to engage, when to redirect, and when she would need to temporarily excuse herself for her own emotional well-being. Although I never disclosed my own circumstances, I would later learn Mrs. Pearl had earned enough life experience to recognize the knowledge I shared could only be forged in the fire.

After each conversation, I would pause on the other side of her door, overcome with gratitude. The encouragement I spoke to Mrs. Pearl was the very same truth my own heart needed to hear. I originally thought I was the one ministering to her, but it turned out God was also ministering to my heart through Mrs. Pearl. I still get chills just thinking of the divine connection and timing only an Ephesians 3:20 God could accomplish.

God answered both of our prayers for peace and comfort through one another. I just love how he connected our two hearts! Mrs. Pearl, in her 90s, was still bearing Psalm 92 fruit and was a huge inspiration to me as a godly woman.

"They will still bear fruit in old age;
they will stay fresh and green ..."

—

PSALM 92:14 (NIV).

Mrs. Pearl had given up her home when her husband's care exceeded what she could provide. She flourished despite her circumstances, bearing fresh fruit right where she was planted. Oh, the goodness and mercy of God that transformed both our hearts in that season!

We treasured our unexpected friendship until Mrs. Pearl passed into the arms of Jesus a few years later. Her fruit blossomed until her last breath, and I am forever grateful God crossed our paths and connected our hearts.

Without realizing it, Mrs. Pearl awakened a passion in me. I would later begin mentoring women in emotionally destructive marriages. It was only then that I began to hear the stories of women who were quarantined with an abusive spouse with nowhere to escape.

Although I longed to be quarantined at home, I was safe, which was one of God's greatest mercies for me and my children. They thrived in virtual school, gaining the confidence and independence they would need moving forward.

God's plan for me during the pandemic was far superior to any plan I could have devised. God anticipated and carefully met our needs while providing the greatest period of transformation for myself, Mrs. Pearl and my children.

Glory be to God!

Heather Jeffery is a Christian writer, speaker and mentor. Heather is a certified abuse and recovery mental health coach. She is passionate about empowering women with biblical truth as they link arms to seek clarity along the recovery journey. Heather believes our stories are meant to be shared to encourage others just as we are encouraged by those in the Bible. God is still at work in our stories now just as He was then. Heather lives in Maryland with her two daughters and loves spending time outdoors, preferably near water. To receive truth-filled encouragement, subscribe at www.heatherjeffery.com or connect with Heather on Instagram @straightenyourcrown.1.

17

No Fear in Love

By Sarah Keeling

> *"There is no fear in love,*
> *but perfect love casts out fear.*
> *For fear has to do with punishment,*
> *and whoever fears*
> *has not been perfected in love."*
>
> ---
>
> **1 JOHN 4:18 (ESV)**

B roken parents.
Broken brother.

Broken everything.

That's what it felt like in my young heart.

It wasn't easy growing up with a single mom and a brother with major disabilities. My sweet mom was amazing. She did the very best she could in the circumstances.

When I was 11 or 12, I became friends with someone at school who led me away from God. I spent the night at her house a few times, and she showed me pornography videos. I was simultaneously and equally curious and grossed out.

I desperately needed someone to talk to about what I saw. I didn't even try to talk to my mom about it because I was embarrassed. Plus, I had seen her broken. I mean really broken—bawling her eyes out every single night after we went to sleep. I couldn't risk upsetting her even more.

In desperation, I turned to a family friend. A neighbor. Someone who had invested in my life over the years. He had been a father figure to me, and he was someone that my mom trusted. Instead of leading me back to my mom for guidance, he chose to exploit me and the situation. I think, in his mind, this was a green light, an opportunity that was too good to pass up.

He began to invite me over for special dinners, "just the two of us," when his wife was out of town. He showed me pornography magazines, and then videos. He answered all of my questions in detail. Then it became time to try out some of the things in the videos. He encouraged me to touch his privates (through his clothes). I remember the effect it had on him.

I'm not sure how long this went on. Maybe months? I'm also not sure what the turning point was, but something happened. I knew things had gone too far, and I went home and told my mom just a little bit about it. I remember her outrage, and I was so relieved that she believed me and was on my side.

I never went back. I stuffed that memory so far down that I didn't think about it for years. It was always there, but I downplayed it in my mind. I was so ashamed because I had been curious and, in my understanding, totally complicit in my mind.

It wasn't until years later that I learned that children are never complicit in sexual abuse, and that's exactly what this was. This person who was supposed to care for me totally violated that trust. He took away a precious gift that God had given me—right, undistorted views about the way God intended intimacy to be and the ability to love someone as God intended.

The Tragic Outcome

After Ty and I got married, these issues started surfacing. Intimacy was always painful, and I could not understand why. We lived in his home-town, and I didn't have any close friends there that I felt I could confide in. Most of my close college friends were also married. They seemed to have wonderful, exciting, intimate relationships with their husbands. I couldn't understand why my body wouldn't cooperate.

I remember thinking, *I wish I had someone I could talk to about this.* A friend, or a mentor. But I was too ashamed, and it seemed like some-thing that was not okay to talk about in church. These were all lies of the enemy. He doesn't want us to bring dark things out into the light. He exercises power by keeping them hidden. Because once they are in the light, they don't seem so scary, and we realize that God's power is way bigger than our mess.

After a while, I began to avoid intimacy as much as possible. Then I would cry because of how much it hurt and how alone I felt. After a pe-riod of over a year with no intimacy, I finally broke down and talked to my husband about it. We went to counseling, and the therapist referred me to a doctor and physical therapist who specialize in sexual disorders.

I had basically experienced PTSD every time Ty would initiate intima-cy. I had to relearn that intimacy was safe and rewire my brain to work through the panic.

I was terrified of intimacy. I mean really terrified. Ty knew this, so he felt terrible for needing intimacy. It was such a difficult time for us.

God's Amazing Redemption

I remember reading a fictional historical romance where the heroine had to marry the local doctor to save her reputation. They were both Christians and agreed, so it worked out, but as she fell in love with him, she was still terrified of intimacy. She repeated the verse to herself, "There is no fear in love," and God helped her overcome her fear.

That verse encouraged me so much during this time. I felt God's agape love—his unconditional, unending, unimaginable love, and that helped me persevere and overcome my fear. God restored our marriage, and now it is better than I could have ever imagined.

It wasn't until years later that I started to remember some of the trauma I had experienced, and the pieces began to fall into place in my mind. I was so ashamed because I had always blamed myself. I felt like it was my fault too! But now I know that my abuser was a child predator who groomed and manipulated me and totally took advantage of my innocence.

I remember the first time I shared with my Bible study group a little bit about what had happened. A sweet friend shared this verse with me:

"There is therefore now no condemnation for those who are in Christ Jesus. For the law of the Spirit of life has set you free in Christ Jesus from the law of sin and death."

—

ROMANS 8:1-2 (ESV)

There is no condemnation. There is no shame.

For years I lived in self-imposed condemnation and shame, but God has delivered me from that. He has taken that away from me!

As soon as I voiced my childhood abuse out loud, I immediately experienced so much freedom. I could seriously feel the burden being lifted off my shoulders. Through it all, I learned this: We have an enemy. He is real. He wants us to be tied up in our past hurts. He doesn't want us to experience freedom in Christ, because once we do, we get really dangerous to him and his schemes.

Now that I have experienced the power of God's perfect love, I want it even more. I want Him to take every single piece of my heart. Every single burden that I cannot carry. Every single doubt. Every single fear. Because it's true that "perfect love casts out fear."

Sarah Keeling is a wife and mother of two boys. She loves Jesus and is passionate about helping others connect deeply with Him and teaching families how to pray the Psalms. She is an advocate for the Bibleless, and she loves encouraging others by sharing what God is doing in her life. She is the author of *Psalm Prayers for Kids* and *Psalm Prayers for the Nations*, and she hosts a podcast called Hearts at Rest with Sarah Keeling. Sarah recently released a new free study, *Finding Jesus in the Psalms*, which helps families connect with Jesus through the book of Psalms.

18

Abraham's Sacrifice - It Happened to Me:

A Divine Test of Faith

By LaVonda McCullough

"Trust in the LORD with all your heart;
do not depend on your own understanding.
Seek his will in all you do,
and he will show you which path to take."

—

PROVERBS 3:5-6 (NLT)

"*She's going to die.*" These words repeatedly echoed in my mind like a ringing bell. My heart was beating so fast that I felt a pulsing sensation in my ears. These were not the words I wanted to hear from the pediatrician. Surely, she was mistaken.

My mind goes back to a moment in time when one of my dear friends from Bible study came for a visit to drop off baby gifts, and she overheard our baby girl coughing. She was one of my most supportive and loving friends throughout my pregnancy. She suggested that my husband and I take our daughter to a close friend, a retired pediatrician who could help us.

At that point, our 8-week-old baby was weak from continuous coughing that had lasted nearly two weeks. Each spell brought anxiety and emotions crashing over me like violent waves. I knew something was seriously wrong, but no one could tell me exactly what. We were about to find out.

The diagnosis was pertussis—whooping cough. My heart sank, and I felt like an elephant was sitting on me, suffocating my last ounce of strength. This highly contagious respiratory disease, caused by the bacterium Bordetella pertussis, was the cause of the uncontrollable violent cough that made her body limp like a wet rag.

The doctor's mouth was moving, but I couldn't process anything.

She said, "I invented the vaccine for this disease." Then I heard her say: "Could you follow these instructions?"

Isn't it amazing how God brings you in contact with the right people at the right time? He is a God of purpose. There I was, standing in a room with the woman who had invented the vaccine for the illness that had killed millions. She knew the medication that could possibly save our baby's life!

I needed a miracle, and I began to repeat in my mind, *she will live and not die; by His stripes, she is healed.*

"I'm so sorry; there is no cure; prepare for the worst, and make her as comfortable as possible," were the last words I can remember the doctor saying as the salty tears streamed down my face.

Going Through the Motions

Following the doctor's instructions, I bundled up our daughter and immediately drove to Eggleston's Children's Hospital in Atlanta. We needed to have her tested and confirmed for pertussis so the hospital could notify authorities of a possible outbreak.

In infants, whooping cough is fatal because air has to be forced into their tiny lungs. A deep inhale is necessary, and she did not have the strength. Each cough was like a noose around her neck.

The nurse demonstrated how to care for her with each coughing spell.

Many thoughts dominated my mind: *Why would the God of love give me this precious gift and take her away? What did I do wrong? Was I not a good mother? Was there some sin in my life?*

The ride home was quiet. I didn't want her to cough. That would make this nightmare real.

We took shifts staying awake to watch her breathe, and if she coughed, we would attempt to force oxygen inside her lungs.

Each cough seemed to last for an eternity.

I had to choose, would I believe the report of the doctor ... or the Bible? The scripture says, "He personally carried our sins in his body on the cross so that we can be dead to sin and live for what is right. By his wounds you are healed" (1 Peter 2:24 NLT).

A few days later, the Center for Disease Control and Prevention representatives were at our door. They had a long list of questions for my husband and me.

I wanted to escape what felt like an interrogation. I was exhausted mentally, physically and, yes, spiritually. I started to flip pages in my Bible to find comfort and peace.

I found: "And we know that God causes everything to work together for the good of those who love God and are called according to his purpose for them" (Romans 8:28 NLT).

Do all things work together for my good? I pondered. *How could good come out of losing my child? How could good come out of the pain that had invaded my world?* A myriad of other questions floated through my mind. It felt like the ground around me was quicksand, drowning me in an abyss.

I blamed myself for so many disappointments in life. Blame led to fear and then anxiety. I began living that vicious cycle all over again in my mind.

How could this be? I go to Bible study weekly and do all the "right" things, such as attending church, serving at the food bank and volunteering.

Then it hit me; God revealed that I was going through the motions but lacked deep roots. I had never allowed myself to go deep and feel the void with Christ. No wonder fear and anxiety surfaced repeatedly.

Startled, I realized that now the means to fill the void was the child, and I wasn't deeply rooted in Christ.

A Moment of Surrender

Then, I heard the Holy Spirit say, *"Give her to me."*

What? I thought. *What does that mean?* And flipping forward, I landed on the page of scripture where Abraham was sacrificing Isaac.

Wow! The Holy Spirit was speaking directly to me; it was as if the words jumped off the page and pierced my heart. Tears began to stream down my face. I was overcome with the presence of God and His clear instructions.

I lifted her from her cradle and fully surrendered my heart, life and child to Him, and the peace that filled the room blanketed me as if I was snuggling in His arms.

Lessons from Light in the Darkness

The good news is our daughter recovered from whooping cough and continued to thrive as an infant. It was later confirmed that she had an allergic reaction to pertussis in the DTP vaccine administered as part of her infant shot series. Adrienne is now a healthy young woman who enjoys mentoring teens and sharing the love of Jesus.

As I reflect on this challenging time, several invaluable reminders come to mind:

- I must trust God with everything; He alone is the source to fill the void in my life. Fulfillment does not come from my husband, children, career or social status.
- This trial renewed my mind with the power of God's Word and opened my mouth as a weapon to speak life. Internalizing scripture to connect my head to my heart was necessary and required spending time to develop an intimate relationship with God.
- Challenging situations can become opportunities to give glory to

God. I can refocus if I stop looking at what is happening in the phys-ical—heartache, sickness, financial hardship, piles of dirty dishes—and focus on the spiritual and the eternal.

- The Bible tells us that some breakthroughs come only through fast-ing and praying. Developing these disciplines and incorporating them into my lifestyle brought lasting change.

In the midst of my mental and spiritual health struggle, the darkness was overwhelming at times, and I could not see the light. I felt con-sumed by anxiety and fear. But God's love and faithfulness restored my faith and gave me hope. If I had not experienced this trauma, my rela-tionship with God would have remained shallow and based on perfor-mance, not on intimacy that came from deep roots, along with the abil-ity to hear and know God intimately for myself, as I never had before.

Dr. LaVonda McCullough is a Christian life coach special-izing in empowering women with a Christian approach. She has coached countless women to complete freedom through the Christian discipline of Daily Quiet Time. As the founder of Joyful Journey, LaVonda enjoys hosting her an-nual RefresHER retreat, which allows women to experience how to discern the voice of the Holy Spirit, develop an inti-mate relationship with God and share their divine encounter. As a woman who has experienced shame, trauma, loss and depression, she offers a deeper understanding of healing through prayer and forgiveness. A recent empty-nester, she has been married to her college sweetheart for 33 years, and together they have three adult children.

19

Finding Contentment in the Midst of Suffering

By Kari Minter

> *"... I have learned to be content in whatever circumstances I find myself."*
>
> ---
>
> **PHILIPPIANS 4:11 (CSB)**

L ife has a funny way of twisting and turning when you least expect it. Several years ago, I was knocked off my feet by one of the biggest twists I've ever faced. Had God not stepped into my mess and spoken clearly, recovery would not have been possible.

The year 2019 brought with it a dreamy life. I had successfully transitioned my kids from homeschool to public school, my husband was leading a rapidly growing church we loved, and I was living my dream role of writing Christian curriculum while developing a women's ministry. Plus, our best friends lived just a few blocks away, which meant there was always a backyard hangout, spontaneous pizza nights or a random bike ride occurring. Life was good.

Until a random Tuesday afternoon.

My husband came home from work, sharing that an elder had voiced concern about me, as the lead pastor's wife, having so much influence in the church. The recommendation was that I quit leading, teaching, speaking or mentoring women. To type that statement seems so void of emotion, but it was the opposite of emotionless. The debate over my role lasted for months behind closed doors and isolated me from members of my community.

Sometimes standing against adversity is easy. This was not one of those times. The harsh words, false accusations and resulting isolation wounded my soul in a way I've never felt before or since. When there's a lack of community, the enemy gains his foothold. And his foothold took its toll on me emotionally and, eventually, physically.

This unfortunate incident birthed a narrative of destruction in my brain. I began believing I was unwanted, and my giftings and personality were, at best, too much for other people and, at worst, sin. The stress involved in coping with this attack began wrecking my physical health. It kept my body at such a high level of inflammation that no amount of steroid shots, diet changes or physical therapy could ease the pain. Every step a doctor took to alleviate pain only made things worse. I went from active and social to secluded and stationary.

What began as back pain turned into migraines, which turned into medical tests and a whole host of issues with my body. The words "multiple sclerosis" and "your body no longer has an immune system" were thrown around aimlessly as I visited specialist after specialist. Each new doctor's office brought with it a glimmer of hope that maybe, just maybe, this doctor would have a cure. Instead, the visits usually ushered in more side effects from medicines and intensified the pain.

Then our best friends walked away, a loss that fed into the narrative that I was too much for people. The emotional scars became challenging to deal with as the physical pain pushed me more and more into isolation.

But here's the thing about God. Often he uses the brokenness of the world and our bodies to change our perspective.

A few years into this chronic physical pain and emotional turmoil journey, I walked into a hotel room and became violently ill. Alone on a hotel bathroom floor, scared and miserable, I felt the presence of the Lord overcome me. At that moment, I felt God asking, "Is my presence enough for you?"

I had spent years looking for healing. I had seen every doctor and tried every supplement and medicine. I changed my diet and eating habits. I'd gone to counseling to help with the emotional stress. I was doing everything I knew to do in an attempt to get my life back to the normal I had once experienced. Hours were spent journaling and begging God for healing. I searched the scriptures to find hope while waiting for life to return to normal. And now, lying on the bathroom floor, I felt the Lord asking me if He was enough. If suffering was my new normal, was He enough?

Immediately Philippians 4:11 popped into my mind: "I have learned to be content in whatever circumstances I find myself."

Content? I thought. *How can I be content to suffer for the rest of my life? To not be the mom or wife I want to be? How does that even work, God?*

Suddenly, I had an indescribable need to hear Philippians 4 in context. I turned on the audio Bible and heard:

"Rejoice in the Lord always. I will say it again: Rejoice!" (4:4)

"The Lord is near." (4:5)

"Don't worry ... present your requests to God." (4:6)

"... the peace of God ... will guard [you] ..." (4:7)

"... dwell on these things." (4:8)

These verses come before Paul states, "I have learned the secret of being content" (4:11 NIV). Paul isn't describing contentment as a false emotion convincing us to deny the hardships of life. Instead, it's the result of changing our focus, shifting our perspective from ourselves to God, and rejoicing that God is near and we can lay our burdens at His feet.

For so long, my focus had been on my circumstances. *If only I could forgive, eliminate the anger, find the right combination of medicine to stop the pain and be the active mom I desired.* Without realizing it, I had become the center of my world. Emotional and physical pain can force you to think about yourself way too much. At that moment on the bathroom floor, as I listened to the verse in context, I began confessing that, without even realizing it, emotional and physical healing had become my idol. Contentment and peace are impossible if your focus is on idols, not God.

As my eyes shifted heavenward, my heart did as well.

"Yes, God," I prayed. "If this is the life that You've given me, I will continue to rejoice in You because You are near."

I released the struggle and idolatry of chasing personal healing and embraced my Father in Heaven. Immediately my soul found peace, even though my body continued to suffer.

Life doesn't immediately get easier after moments like this. Chronic pain tries to make you question God's goodness. It asks, "If God is good, why does He continue to allow me to suffer?" But practicing rejoicing instead of focusing on the pain, memorizing scripture instead of googling the latest medical treatments, and releasing my worries to God instead of only begging Him to heal them changed my perspective.

God alone is my gift while I walk in this world. My body is not my gift. My emotional health is not my gift. God is my gift, and His presence truly is enough.

There's a brokenness in this world and a brokenness in my body. One day all God's children will be resurrected and perfected in Christ, but for the here and now, as we live in the brokenness, God has given us His presence. And His presence is more than enough.

Kari Minter is a pastor's wife, mother of three teenagers, author and Bible teacher who is passionate about helping people cultivate a deeper walk with God. With over a decade of experience teaching and a master's in theological studies from Midwestern Baptist Theological Seminary, Kari is known for her deep insight delivered in a helpful and practical way. Her first traditionally published Bible study, entitled *Beyond Egypt: Learning to Walk in the Freedom of the Exodus*, will be released through Hosanna Revival in January 2024. In addition to this study, she has self-published several studies and teaches an online course entitled Next Step Now. Connect with Kari on her website, Instagram, Facebook or Twitter.

20

Testimony of God Transforming My Life:

I Can Do All Things Through Christ

By Karen O'Reilly

> *"I can do all things through Christ who strengthens me."*
>
> ---
>
> **PHILIPPIANS 4:13 (NKJV)**

Hello, my name is Karen, and I hope to encourage you with my story of how God has transformed and continues to transform my life.

I grew up in a family where my parents were good evangelical Christians, and we attended a Baptist church every Sunday. My dad even served as a youth group leader for a time, and I was so proud of him.

At age 10, I had an awesome Sunday school teacher who explained that we need a savior because it is impossible not to sin. Even at that young age, I understood that I can never, ever be holy enough to come into God's presence. So, I knelt down on the floor and invited Jesus to come into my heart, and from that moment, my life was transformed!

However, our world came crashing down around my teenage years. My dad had a few tough financial years and lost his way to God. We lost our home twice, once in a fire and the second time because my dad couldn't pay the mortgage. Then, I discovered that he had been continuously unfaithful to my mum.

That was a lot for a young teenager to cope with, but I was mightily blessed because Jesus Christ was and continues to be my anchor.

During my adolescence and into my early twenties, I leaned heavily on God. I loved reading His Word and listening to worship songs on my Walkman. I had many decisions to make, including moving out of my parents' home and going to nursing school. I had no money, but I sure did see many miracles of provision!

I was able to live in the nurses' home for a time, and throughout my training, I was also part of the workforce. The money earned from working shifts in the hospital paid for my uniform, books and accommodation.

God spoke to me loudly through scripture during this time. He even provided a unique way for me to carry it along as I worked.

Our nurses' uniform was very old-fashioned, based on Florence Nightingale. I had to wear a navy blue polka-dot dress with a starched white cotton apron. The straps crossed over on my back, and I secured the straps to the waist of the apron with nappy pins!

But that apron naturally provided a space between the bib and my dress, and that was where I could safely store my notebook and scripture cards throughout my shift. Whenever I got overwhelmed, I would whip out scripture and pray through it.

My favorite scripture to get me through a shift was Philippians 4:13: "I can do all things through Christ who strengthens me." I still hold on tight to that verse!

As an adult, I had to make my own way in life, and I knew that I could never go home. I remember having a good chat with God. I knew that the boy I was dating wasn't passionate about God, so I broke off our friendship. I told God I was ready to meet my husband, and I didn't want to waste any more time dating. The next man I dated was to be my husband, and he had to want to be trained as a pastor or church minister!

God answered my prayers and brought a young, handsome man into my life, who later pursued his calling to train for the Anglican Church ministry.

My life has not been without its challenges, but I credit God for seeing me through them all. About four years ago, I asked God what He wanted me to do next, and I kept hearing the words "scriptural grace" during my prayer time. Through much prayer, I discovered that God was leading me to write topical Bible reading plans and devotional Bible studies that have the power to transform people from the inside out.

Looking back on my life, I marvel at how I can see God's fingerprints all over it. I know that if you surrender your life to God and trust Him to place His good plans in your heart and life, you too will look back and marvel at how God guides you through those twisty curved bends in your life, and how He truly can make your path straight.

My favorite Hebrew name for God is El Roi, which means the God who sees me. We discover this name of God in Genesis 16:14-15. We meet Hagar, an Egyptian slave who encountered God in the desert after she had run away from her mistress, Sarah. Hagar was a slave who had been sexually used and verbally abused. She was a woman amazed that God had heard her cries and had seen her misery.

I want to encourage you to seek God with all your heart and trust Him with your life. Seek His presence throughout your day and in all the decisions that you have to make. Don't ever forget this scriptural truth: Just as God saw Hagar, He sees you in every situation that you encounter. God sees your pain, confusion and suffering. He is right there with you when you feel abandoned or think that no one cares about you.

You are God's precious child, and He does indeed have good plans for you (Jeremiah 29:11). So, I want to wrap up my testimony by calling you to surrender your life to God and to trust Him with your future. Just like me, you can look back on your life and marvel at how God has guided you through the twists and turns of life, making your path straight.

God bless, Karen.

Karen O'Reilly is the writer, creator and designer of Scriptural Grace and lives in the southeast of Ireland. She designs products using scripture to encourage you to live an intentional Christ-centered life. Karen is passionate about scripture and writes about growing your faith through Bible studies and reading plans. Her passion is in unlocking the hidden treasures tucked away in scripture that are sometimes missed at first glance, and in helping apply its transformative power to your life. She is currently writing and praying through the Bible in chronological order and

21

Shattered Dreams Can Be a Gift from God:
Trusting God When You Don't Understand His Ways

By Stacey Pardoe

"Trust in the LORD with all your heart and lean not on your own understanding..."

—

PROVERBS 3:5 (NIV)

The afternoon sunbeams slanted sideways through the window the day I received the phone call. After years of pursuing my dream job as a professional writer, I finally landed a huge writing project. My future with the company looked promising. If everything went well, I could easily make a career out of writing.

Then, only eight months after signing the contract and pouring my heart into multiple writing projects with the company, a very different phone call changed the course of my career. Due to my biblical core values, the company decided to terminate me. Forever. No second chances.

In an instant, my writing career was dashed before my eyes. The projects I had poured my heart into for eight long months were terminated as well. I felt like I'd been punched in the ribs.

Reeling with pain, I reflected on the sacrifices our family had made—planning vacations around writing deadlines and fighting for balance while I lay awake at night pondering ideas and investing my whole heart into pursuing my dream.

I felt angry, betrayed, embarrassed and, mostly, heartbroken.

On a cloudy autumn evening a few days after receiving the crushing news, I went to the woods to sort through my feelings with God. Alone in the forest, I poured out every emotion, weeping and asking Him why He had allowed my dream to be stamped out.

As a golden aspen leaf fluttered to my feet in the breeze, familiar words came to mind: "Trust in the LORD with all your heart and lean not on your own understanding" (Proverbs 3:5 NIV).

I sensed God asking me to trust Him with what I could not yet understand.

Most likely, you've walked through devastating losses too. Maybe, like me, you know how it feels to watch a lifelong dream burn to ashes right in front of you. Perhaps your heart broke as a loved one lost a battle with a terminal disease, or maybe you're still reeling over a prodigal child, a shattered marriage, a miscarriage or a betrayal from someone you trusted.

In these moments, it's tempting to let bitterness creep into our lives. It's tempting to take offense at God for allowing the pain. However, our loving Father has a different invitation for us. He invites us to trust Him with the parts of our stories we cannot yet understand.

As I held the golden aspen leaf in my hand, I whispered the following prayer: "Jesus, I don't understand what you are doing, but I trust You."

The prayer didn't push the grief out of my heart. I was still disappointed, sad and confused. However, the anger was replaced with the peace that passes understanding.

God's Redemption

A few months after my writing career came to a screeching halt, my 11-year-old daughter Bekah approached me with an interesting request.

"Mom, can we write a mother-daughter devotional book together?" she asked.

"Sure, babe," I answered. In the back of my mind, I didn't expect the idea to come to fruition.

Despite my doubts, Bekah was persistent. She started writing and invited me to join her. One devotion turned into ten, and within a few months, we had written a 258-page book with 60 devotions for moms and daughters to read together.

Not long after we finished the book and published it together, I went for a walk beneath the same aspen trees where I had wrestled with God just a year earlier. As a golden leaf fell to the ground, I had a full-circle moment.

For the first time, I realized that I wouldn't have had time to undertake the once-in-a-lifetime process of writing a book with my daughter if I had continued writing for the company that terminated me.

All along, God knew that Bekah would ask me to write a book with her. He knew it would be one of the most cherished experiences of our lives. He knew that writing just one book with my girl was worth far more than writing 100 books as a professional writer. As I reflected on our time working together, I knew I wouldn't trade the experience with my girl for anything—even a career as a professional writer.

Your dream might have fallen apart. Perhaps you've been trying to bring it to life for decades, but God hasn't opened the right door. Maybe you poured your whole heart into an endeavor that didn't work out. You're frustrated, and you don't understand what God is doing.

With all the compassion in my heart, let me gently encourage you today. When God closes a door in your life, you can trust that He is capable of opening another door—a better one.

God will fulfill his purpose in our lives. He is worthy of our trust. His ways are higher than ours, and His plans are better than ours.

You might not trust God with your uncertain situation just yet. That's okay. Today, will you take the first step toward trusting Him by praying this prayer? "Father, I don't understand what You are doing. Please help me to trust You with what I cannot understand."

This is a prayer your Father in Heaven will answer.

Stacey Pardoe spends her days exploring wild places with her three children, cleaning up messes and writing words in the fringe hours. She lives in western Pennsylvania, where she is a wife, mentor and teacher with a master's degree in education. She writes weekly at staceypardoe.com. Stacey and her 12-year-old daughter, Bekah, recently published a one-of-a-kind mother-daughter devotional entitled Girl to Girl: 60 Devotions for a Closer Relationship and Deeper Faith.

22

Royal Steps:
Living as God's Chosen People
By Susan Park

Growing up as a Korean American, I felt disconnected from the ancient Korean palaces and Korean royalty seen in history books or in historical Korean dramas. I was more familiar with the White House or with Princes William and Harry.

However, during my last visit to South Korea, I began to appreciate the legacy and beauty of ancient Korean royalty as I walked through Changdeokgung Palace. Colorful Korean palaces stood tall, surrounded by grand courtyards. I walked through the Secret Garden of Changdeokgung Palace, where lush greenery and ponds with lilies paved the ancient roads. I imagined a Korean king or queen walking the same beautiful paths many centuries ago. I wondered what their lives were like as they enjoyed the privileges of their position, which was a far cry from my upbringing in a small suburb of Chicago.

My childhood home didn't have a secret garden. However, there were lilac bushes that bloomed every spring, covering the metal fence dividing the backyard and street. I can still remember the smell of the lilac bushes as I played in the backyard with my younger sisters. Even though there were happy childhood memories associated with the lilac bushes, one painful memory stands out.

When I was in elementary school, I was often bullied and left out by my peers. I was one of the few Korean Americans in the area, and as a minority and a shy girl, it was difficult for me to fit in. I remember sitting alone at lunch or playing by myself on the school playground. My parents were busy working, so I had no one to confide in about my struggles. I felt lonely and wondered why the other girls wouldn't include me in their social groups.

One spring day, I was in my kitchen with the back screen door open. The lilac bushes were in full bloom, and it was beautiful outside. I had come home from school and was enjoying an afternoon snack when I heard some girls shouting outside my backyard. I couldn't see who was shouting since the lilac bushes were blocking the view. As I peered out of the back screen door, the shouting became clearer. It sounded like it was coming from a group of girls from my school. They were yelling out curses at me from behind the lilac bushes as they walked past my backyard!

My heart broke into a million pieces.

Throughout my childhood and teenage years, I often struggled with low self-esteem and was afraid of rejection from others. I had a hard time accepting myself and carried much hurt in my heart. I had emotional breakdowns and became depressed and anxious. When my mom noticed my emotional breakdowns, she became worried. She arranged for different pastors to talk to me.

Then one day, one of the pastors shared the gospel with me, and I accepted Christ!

After I accepted Christ, my faith grew in Him. I sensed His presence and learned more about Him through my youth group and during my college years. I started understanding His deep love for me and how He was always faithful. God brought life-giving friendships into my life. He started healing my broken heart with His unconditional love for me. I found great comfort in the fact that He would never reject me the way others did in the past.

One day, when I came upon the verse from 1 Peter 2:9 about Christians being a "royal priesthood," that phrase caught my attention. As someone who identified with being unworthy, the word "royal" did not seem to convey who I was. I thought that word was only reserved for people who were popular, beloved or born into a royal family.

However, as my relationship with God grew, I understood and accepted that I am worthy through the blood of Christ. I am His beloved child and royal daughter because God is my Father and King! Also, I belong to a larger royal family of God with other brothers and sisters in Christ.

As we do life together, we can walk with God despite the rejection that occurs behind the lilac bushes of our lives. We have hope for eternal life that far exceeds the fancy palaces and secret gardens of this world. As I walk through this life with its ups and downs, one truth remains constant: I am a royal daughter of God who walks hand-in-hand with a Father and King, both now and forever.

Susan Park is a Korean American Christian writer. She loves to encourage God's women with words of hope and joy. She is currently working on her first novel about a second-generation Korean American college woman set in the 1990s. She was a contributing writer and assistant copy editor for the Christian online magazine, *Marked Ministry*. Susan was a speaker about creativity at The Extraordinary Faith Summit and a contributing writer for the Dawn Bible app. She has been a featured writer and podcast guest for other Christian writers. Susan lives in the Chicago area with her husband and three boys. Connect with Susan through her website, susanepark.com and on Instagram, Facebook or Pinterest @susaneparkwrites.

23

Devastating Loss Leads to Eternal Gain:
Redeeming Grief

By Elise Daly Parker

> *"... I consider everything a loss*
> *because of the surpassing worth*
> *of knowing Christ Jesus my Lord,*
> *for whose sake I have lost all things.*
> *I consider them garbage,*
> *that I may gain Christ."*
>
> —
>
> **PHILIPPIANS 3:8 (NIV)**

U p until I was about 30 years old, my faith was shallow and immature. If I needed something, I sent up a request in hopes God would respond.

Then my faith was tested.

We never imagined being pregnant with two babies. And we were absolutely ecstatic upon receiving the news. Then, at only five months, I went into labor. When my water broke, there was no stopping the inevitable delivery of these precious tiny babies, too underdeveloped to live outside my womb.

The twins had felt like a gift from God. Then the loss felt like the worst kind of cruelty. I felt set up—brought to the heights only to be thrown into the depths. I wondered, *What kind of terrible God would allow such suffering? How could this be happening? What have I done wrong?*

I was angry, hurt and sad. I felt distant from this God whom I had trusted in my youth and innocence. Starting in middle school, through my journal, I poured out my heart to God about confusing feelings and relationships—with my parents, siblings and friends. I shared my agony over (and obsession with) boys, my "crush of the month." In my loneliest hours, I prayed to my version of God—big, high-up-in-the-sky, far away.

Since I believed God is in charge of our birth and death, who else could I blame but God when I lost those babies?

In the weeks after my loss, I wrestled with my faith and kept my distance from God. I didn't speak directly to Him because I felt I couldn't honestly share my feelings. This was too dangerous, disrespectful, irreverent ... intimate.

These feelings were jumbled up inside, and I didn't know what to do with them. My stepmother, Jane, a woman I admire for her deep faith, encouraged me: "It's okay to be angry with God. It's okay to tell Him—He can take it."

For the first time in my life, I had permission to be real with God. I tiptoed into this new territory at first. But eventually, the dam broke. My hot tears poured out, along with a flood of emotions—anger, disbelief, devastation, disappointment, betrayal. Yes, of course, this was about my babies, but it was also about trying to understand, *Who is this God?* Up to this point, I had envisioned Him a bit like a rabbit's foot.

Now, life had thrown me a gut punch. And since I had permission to be real, I had questions. *Where were you, God, when I was so desperate to keep those babies? How could you let something so bad happen if you're so good? Why would you set me up for such joy only to let me down with such despair? Do you hate me? Because right now, it feels that way!*

I wanted to end my relationship with God. I threatened to leave Him. But as I poured out my heart, I somehow felt Him near. In my own strength, I was unable to overcome this loss. I had no resources for coping and reasoning my way through this.

I had gotten to the end of myself ... and there, I found God. His Spirit within me gave me comfort, the beginnings of peace. Some kind of inexplicable blessed assurance surfaced.

A little begrudgingly, over time, I drew closer to God. But we were still on shaky ground.

When I was about five months pregnant again, my husband was painting every room in our little house. So I went to stay with my sister a few blocks away to avoid the fumes. When I arrived, she was emptying the dishwasher; her one-year-old was in a high chair, and her four-year-old was coloring at the kitchen table.

My heart was pained by their family bliss.

She looked up brightly, "Hey, Leesie! Want to come to Bible study with me?" She had recently joined a vibrant nondenominational church.

"No, thanks."

"Oh, come on. I think you'll like it. God is so good."

"Easy for you to say. You have your two babies," I muttered. I didn't want to be a downer. But at that moment, I couldn't help myself.

I was definitely curious but afraid of the unknown. I pushed past my resistance and went to the Bible study. A roomful of young women welcomed me. After the lesson, the leader asked us to share our faith story: "When did you come to know Jesus?" I felt a little defensive, not sure what a faith story was. "I've known Jesus for as long as I can remember."

The conversation then shifted to an upcoming retreat. I could use more of the community and support this group readily shared. So, I signed up.

The name of the retreat was "Are You Living Like an Orphan or a

Daughter of the King?"[1] About 15 of us gathered for inspiring worship, talks and group sessions. I realized that, in fact, I *was* living like an orphan, as though I'd been abandoned, not at all like a beloved daughter of my Heavenly Father.

After lunch, I welcomed some time for quiet reflection. It was March in New Jersey, cold and a bit gray, but no snow. At five months pregnant, I felt strong, healthy and a little antsy. So, I bundled up to take a walk in the fresh air. I came upon a large open field. It was quiet, serene. The sun broke through the clouds, and suddenly, I felt clarity, warmth and peace flow through my mind and body. It felt like I had been hit by a bolt of energy! I felt joy for the first time in a very long time. I didn't see God, but I knew He was there. The words "I believe!" burst through my thoughts.

I skipped back to my room, eager to share with my sister this amazing God encounter. I held my Bible, pointing to it, exclaiming, "I believe. I don't know what I believe. But I believe it all!" God's Word took on a whole new meaning as I read it regularly—words full of life, timeless, a record of God's love story to His people and, also, directly to me.

My pain and sorrow led me to the foot of the cross, where Jesus became real and personal. God's Word became my anchor, a beacon, a map. The Bible opened my mind to the knowledge I lacked, infused with the Spirit I desperately needed. It was a new day.

When I lost the twins, I found God in a way that forever changed my life. Did I have to lose so much to gain an intimate relationship with the Lord? I will never know this side of Heaven. But I am eternally grateful for the way God met me in my sorrow and has continued to meet me in my joys and sorrows since.

(1) Based on the book, *From Fear to Freedom: Living as Sons and Daughters of God* by Rose Marie Miller, who was the retreat speaker.

Elise Daly Parker is a certified life coach, writer and speaker. She helps women clear the path to a life they love, with a particular focus on helping moms savor, not just survive, seasons of motherhood with clarity, confidence and calm. Elise has been married for 38 years, and has four daughters and two sons-in-love, as well as two grandchildren. She shares her life lessons on identity, marriage, momming and relationships with transparency, authenticity and sometimes humor. Elise is the co-author of *Unshakable Peace in an Unsteady World*, available where books are sold. Connect with Elise on her website EliseDalyParker.com and on Instagram and Facebook @EliseDalyParker.

24

Relationship Transformation:

Healing Generational Brokenness

By Jessica L. Peck

"But You, O LORD,
are a shield for me,
My glory and the One who lifts up my head."

—

PSALM 3:3 (NKJV)

I t simply wasn't fair. How could this happen?

My cheeks burned as anger crept across my face and the familiar grip of disappointment enveloped my heart. I longed for reconciliation with my parents as I was becoming a mother myself, but another well-intentioned effort had once again ended with hurtful words and painful wounds.

As the fiery arrows of doubtful questions made their mark, old familiar thoughts entwined their torturous vines through the secret places of my heart. *What's wrong with me? Why can't I just let things go? Why am I always such a disappointment?*

I grew up in what many would view from the outside as an idyllic childhood, but my home was emotionally unhealthy. Past generations of relational traumas made themselves known behind an unforgiving facade of perfection. Unable to imagine life without the illusion, each family member adopted destructive coping mechanisms in the ironic search for survival—alcoholism, substance abuse, unhealthy relationships and isolation, among other open secrets that were clearly seen but never discussed.

My chosen weapon was the most socially acceptable yet perhaps the most damaging of all. I rigidly, and if I'm honest, rabidly adopted an unsustainable standard of perfection and expectation of performance. I somehow thought if my achievements piled up high enough, one day I would be convinced that I was enough. This unrelenting burden of perfection left me unapproachable, unrelatable and just plain unlikeable.

Most of all, it left me feeling very alone and unhappy in the present while still a prisoner of the past.

As my tears spilled over into the night, I found comfort in God's Word: "You have collected all my tears in your bottle. You have recorded each one in your book" (Psalm 56:8 NLT).

My heart began to still before the Lord as I simply asked, "Why?" He gently whispered familiar words from Psalm 84:11: "For the LORD God is a sun and shield; The LORD will give grace and glory; No good *thing* will He withhold From those who walk uprightly" (NKJV).

The truth hit me. My vision of a pathway to a restored relationship that I saw as inherently good, God didn't. He wasn't going to change my path in this journey. He was going to change *me*. Even still, my heart quivered with doubt. Would the Lord really withhold no good thing? Because ... I persisted in my prayer ... how was relationship restoration not a good thing?

Then the Lord of Heaven reminded me He holds nothing back from His beloved: "He who did not spare his own Son but gave him up for us all, how will he not also with him graciously give us all things?" (Romans 8:32 ESV)

How could I believe that God would give His one and only cherished

Son for me, the very best version of good, but unfairly withhold a restored earthly relationship, something infinitely lesser?

He wouldn't. I had to accept that in God's infinite wisdom, restoration of this relationship was simply not a good thing. I had been waiting for Him to do a good work by changing my relationship. Instead, He who began a good work would be faithful to complete it ... by changing *me*.

In time, I've come to see that through the loss of that relationship, God has been faithful to keep His word in the Psalm He sang over me that night.

Like the sun, God lit my path and showed me the way to go. With radiance, He revealed things I had never been in an emotional place to see before. His companionship warmed my spirit. His light illuminated sin in my own life and gently pushed me toward repentance.

Like a shield, God protected me from destructive patterns of communication, words that caused me pain, and unhealthy generational relationship dynamics.

In giving grace, He poured out unmerited favor as I learned to rely on Him to sustain me, walking daily with the Lord on my well-lit and protected path.

In giving glory, He didn't use public adulation or worldly blessings. The Greek word for glory is *doxa*, from which we get doxology, conveying a sense of heavy dignity. It means God gifted me with the literal weight of His presence, a reassuring and steady comfort.

God did not miraculously transform my circumstances. But my heart and mind are transformed when I accept His invitation to walk through an open door to a new way of living—a place in which I intentionally view the present as new and vibrant instead of allowing old habits to build a perpetual memorial to the cruel mirage of the past.

It's hard. Transformation and freedom create environments in which truth is an unwelcome foe to others. It's a world in which you are labeled as the betrayer. The cost of healing on the surface appears to be the loss of everything you hold dear. Only by engaging distance and discipline will you realize you were clinging to disease and destruction.

There are days when I fail. I grieve. I long for the comforts of old chains when I face the future with fear of the unknown. Some days my head hangs low in defeat, and I feel vulnerable and weak. On those days, I grant myself the grace God affords me through new mercies every morning. I celebrate each victory, no matter how small. I remember how far I've come. I journal the ways in which God has shown Himself faithful in protecting my healing heart.

I recognize some relationships may not be healed this side of Heaven, but I trust that one day everything will be made new in a way that I can only see "through a glass, darkly" now. But one day, I will see face to face! "Now I know in part; then I shall know fully, even as I have been fully known" (1 Corinthians 13:12 KJV, ESV).

Praise God from whom all blessings flow!

Dr. Jessica L. Peck has engaged, encouraged, equipped, and empowered families to raise holistically healthy kids as a pediatric nurse practitioner in primary care. A native Texan, she is a clinical professor at the Baylor University Louise Herrington School of Nursing. An internationally award-ed nursing leader, she served as president of the National Association of Pediatric Nurse Practitioners and has received numerous awards for her work. Dr. Peck is the author of the award-winning book *Behind Closed Doors: A Guide for Parents and Teens to Navigate through Life's Toughest Issues*. She has been a guest on The Nurse Practitioner Show on Sirius XM and appeared on CBS, NBC, ABC, and Fox syndicates. She is married to a rocket scientist, the love of her life, and is mother to four amazing kids, the joy of her life.

25

God's Promises, Miracles and Answered Prayers

By Rachel W. Rains

If you had told me as a young girl that I would grow up to live in Nashville and teach country music and pop singers, I would have thought you were crazy. But that is exactly what happened.

Over my 30-plus years as a vocal coach, I would occasionally hear the dreaded words, "You have such a great voice. Why don't you have a singing career?"

Obviously, we could unpack much in the sting of those words, but the short answer is simple: I didn't believe God was calling me to a singing career. And especially not a singing career in the Christian music industry. I did, however, feel a distinct, unique calling to be a Christian in the secular music industry.

Even at the young age of 20, I deeply understood what "was" and "wasn't" my calling. Not to say disappointments didn't occur along the way. But I sensed God calling me to a different, unexpected path to serve His kingdom purpose.

But I Wanted Out

About our eighth year of living in Nashville (2008), I had two voice clients on different record labels experiencing heartbreaking turmoil in their careers. And it broke my heart to watch. So much so, I prayed, "Lord, I do not want to do this anymore." I wanted out—and I wanted out *right then.*

Had I gotten my way, I would have missed out on the tremendous ride the last few years in Nashville afforded me, professionally. And personally. So many blessings to count … but nonetheless, at the time, I identified my situation as hopeless as the Israelites wandering through the desert for what seemed like centuries in search of the Promised Land.

In the early winter of 2013, my only child, Stormy, was hours away at college, and my sweet mama—hundreds of miles away—was grieving the traumatic, recent loss of my daddy. As I gazed out the bedroom window and contemplated life as women of a certain age often do, God reminded me of another deeply rooted calling that He'd placed on my life long ago: the call to write.

Stunned by this revelation of a half-forgotten promise to a girl of 18, I said, "Okay, God. I'm ready. Let's do this!" But nothing is ever as easy as it sounds. Or occurs nearly as fast as we would hope. The path is riddled with twists and turns, detours, and mountains to scale. But deep in my soul, I knew. Something "new" was on the horizon.

Then, in 2018, after years of hoping, praying and wandering in the proverbial desert, I distinctly heard God whisper the words *"Miracles take time."* I sat straight up and said, "Okay God. I'm gonna hold You to Your promise."

Waiting on the Lord

In those waiting years, I learned to relinquish my desire for a controlled outcome and rely on God's perfect plan. And perhaps even more importantly, to trust His *perfect timing*. Finally, during the summer of 2019, I sensed God moving.

Life had grown increasingly complicated over the last several years, and miracles were desperately needed. Without getting too far into the weeds of all the moving parts, I will say I was exhausted from caring for all the people in my life, from afar, who needed care. I simply prayed, "Lord, either move me to I-35 or move those who need care to I-65." I even dared God in a financial matter with the words, "God, it would take a miracle. But You are in the business of miracles."

All I can say is when God moves, friends, He moves at lightning speed. After winding down a life-altering, five-year journey of chasing justice, I accidentally stumbled on a house listing outside my hometown near the Oklahoma-Texas border. It was Monday, January 6, 2020. And it felt as if God said, *"Here is your new house."*

Never in my wildest dreams would I have considered moving back to Oklahoma. Much less to the town where I grew up! It simply didn't make sense.

Hubby hemmed and hawed. What would his new company think? He had just started a new position. A position that would allow us to live anywhere in the South. But moving to the edge of his territory felt a little too dicey at the time. The next morning, he received the call: "We are extending your territory to cover the entire southern portion [coast to coast] of the United States." And do you know what states are in the center of that new territory? Texas. And Oklahoma. Well, friends, that was all the confirmation we needed.

After making the trip to see the house in Hometown, Oklahoma, we immediately put our Nashville house up for sale. Little did we know just 10 days later, my mama would be diagnosed with cancer. Suddenly, I couldn't get to Oklahoma fast enough.

Two more agonizing weeks passed by before we loaded up our belongings, said goodbye to our home of 20-plus years and landed in our new surroundings. And then, four days into our new life, the unthinkable happened.

The world shut down.

We had been too busy packing to notice the rumbling of a pandemic growing overseas.

Miracles Do Happen

If we had flinched the slightest bit during those earliest days of responding to God's prompting, the sale of our home most likely would not have gone through in time for us to land in Oklahoma. Or quite possibly, not at all.

And remember that small business of a financial matter? With the sale of our house, I no longer had to work outside of the home. Had we stayed in Nashville, my coaching business would certainly have experienced extreme peril, if not ruin. Every musician in Nashville and elsewhere was off the road for an entire year. Probably more.

Ten-plus years I waited, standing on God's promise. And here it was, a spectacular miracle! After all that time, God granted me the deepest desires of my heart. I cared for my mama in her final days. I was in proximity to my Stormy Girl in the new, altered reality that the pandemic brought.

And when the dust finally settled, studying His Word and spreading the news of His great love became my new day job! What a faithful God we serve. So full of mercy and grace. And I'm *still* discovering all the miraculous ways God has been faithful in our journey. Too many answered prayers to mention.

It must've been about a year or so after our brutal, sudden departure from Nashville that I noticed heavy traffic in the distance. Across the cow pasture of the neighboring ranch, a mere stone's throw away, sat I-35. It was then the startling realization hit me. Miracles really do take time. And most importantly, God really does hear—and answer—our prayers.

Yes, God is exceedingly faithful. Trust in His goodness, my friends.

Rachel W. Rains accepted Christ around the age of five and was raised in a family deeply rooted in the Christian faith and a few "religious" beliefs. A Nashville vocal technique coach turned writer/speaker, Rachel W. Rains writes about overcoming the struggle to love in a broken, unlovable world. Currently residing outside of her hometown on the Oklahoma-Texas border, Rachel finds tremendous joy encouraging and equipping maturing believers in "Living this one life for Kingdom purpose—and loving fiercely!" Especially through her widely shared campaign, Accept the Love Challenge. Connect with Rachel at rachelwrains.com, on Instagram or on Facebook.

26

Golden Hour:
Savoring the Days We've Been Given
By Ronne Rock

> "They who dwell in the ends of the earth
> stand in awe of Your signs;
> You make the dawn and the sunset shout for joy."
>
> —
>
> **PSALM 65:8 (NASB)**

G olden hour.

It's the inviting liminal space just after sunrise and just before sunset, where the sun bends low and kisses the earth with a soft welcome.

Photographs are richer when taken during the golden hour. Faces glimmer and landscapes dance. I've been awestruck by golden hours in places around the world—skies in Guatemala become radiant as mist moves delicately along mountainsides, and the horizon in Chicago over Lake Michigan is layered in lavender and coral. On a chilly December afternoon in York, England, the golden hour looked like an English country garden of peony, delphinium and violet. I can't help but think about God seeking out image and likeness in Genesis 3:8, while "walking in the cool *misting* shadows of the garden" (VOICE).

Perhaps God finds particular delight in the golden hour too.

For years on my bucket list, you'd find, "Savor a sunrise with my husband on the lake by our home." Sunsets on the lake are calming rituals for us. Sunrises are becoming a tradition too.

The golden hour has become more than a time of day in recent years. The liminal space has revealed an eternal beauty in its presence.

Seeing ... And Being Seen

"This is reality."

I wrote those words in the corner of the journal pages used to document all that we were seeing, smelling, hearing, tasting and feeling as my granddaughter and I sat in a deer stand in the woods of East Texas and watched the quiet way the world around us responded to the wash of color just before sunset reaching through pines.

"We're hunting beauty, GiGi," she said, smiling.

We smelled green and brown and smoke in the distance. We heard crickets, crows and the creaking of wood beneath our feet. We tasted the sweetness of clementines we had packed as snacks, felt the prickle of pine cones and the anticipation of seeing a deer.

On the page marked "I see," I wrote about the way shadowed pine cones in the trees resembled flocks of birds and how the air around us was permeated with a glimmering glow. My granddaughter documented a bunny, the way logger tire tracks make ribbons on the road, and the doe we did indeed see (we named them Felice, Diana and Cocomelon).

—and me.

I saw "GiGi" on her list and fought back tears.

There is something about being seen. Most certainly, it wasn't the goal of our adventure as we donned our camouflaged clothing and jaunted on a four-wheeler to the small wooden fort on stilts. We just wanted to feel brave and hunt beauty and wear lip gloss. But in that golden hour, with no fanfare or location markers to tell the world where we were, the power of presence was balm.

Walking Through the Decades

Years ago, I sent a different sort of list to a woman celebrating her 30th birthday. Entitled "30 Things You Could Learn from a Woman in Her 50s," it included things like the importance of forgiveness and laugh lines, the joy of freshly baked bread slathered with butter, and the value of cowboy boots in a wardrobe.

That list was written a decade ago, with the wisdom available to me at the time.

There was the wisdom of the 20s, in which we learn to pay our own bills and set alarm clocks that jar us into the reality of responsibility. For some of us, the 20s find us reciting vows and rocking babies. For others, the 20s find us picking up pieces of dreams shattered far too quickly. We see every break in the destiny handed to us by the generations that had come before—and we believe we have the mortar to repair them all. In our 20s, we still believe we are invincible.

The wisdom of the 30s was there—a jarring awakening to the "tick-tick-tick" of the second hands on a clock. We feel the pressure to increase speed as we stumble and rise time and time again. We hear the voice whisper, "Run harder," as the 30s drum their fingers on the counter with slight contempt. They are full of expectations, and we run to keep up, to make a name, to be a success. We run to be the best because we believe there is a best.

The 40s were there, with a new and fresh grace. Like the first breeze of spring on cheeks glistening with tears, the 40s invite us to sit and rest because it knows we arrive weary. We are given a glass of cool water and asked to share our day. And there have been so many days by then. We have surely tasted loss and pain. We have surely been afraid. And yet we are here. Our vision changes in the 40s; we discover a softness tucked away in the world where there is no best to be achieved. Yes, grace makes her appearance in the 40s. She holds our hand as we extend it to others. She stands by us as we look in the mirror, and she says, "There is beauty to be found here."

The wisdom of the 50s found its way onto the list as it also finds its way into tender places in our souls. We turn a corner to see that the tick-tick-tick is not a clock at all, but rather a metronome, offering cadence for the days that have passed and the days yet to come. If we lean in and listen, we hear a new whisper that says, "Life is beginning upon beginning and story upon story. Savor them all and let them sink deep within you."

It Is here in the 60s, though, where I have found the eternal beauty of the golden hour. They form a decade marked by the tectonic shift from me as a child to me as a matriarchal orphan. My mother passed away at the age of 62; my father died at 67. I would love to see the 70s or 80s. Yet, the tick-tick-tick has moved from metronome to stopwatch in a life that now feels filled with unknowns. 63 beats the odds. 68 resets the pace.

My grandson asked me, "When do you think you'll go to heaven, GiGi?" I answered, "That's a really great question. I don't know yet."

"Tomorrow is OK. You can wait until tomorrow," he said, smiling.

The liminal space and beauty of the golden hour, with its softness and warmth, has welcomed me in this season.

The golden hour offers just enough light to see and be seen. The golden hour offers just enough time to savor a sunset and eat an orange and take note of every gift of beauty and suffering. The golden hour, offering space to be present, no matter what the days might bring.

The golden hour, whispering the promise of golden hours to come.

Ronne Rock is an author and speaker who offers road-tested wisdom about grace-filled leadership and discovering your God-crafted design and purpose. She travels globally to cultivate stories of transformation with Orphan Outreach. And as a teacher and mentor, Ronne offers writers and other creatives insight on how to safeguard your soul in the marketplace. She is the author of four books, including *One Woman*

Can Change the World: Reclaiming Your God– Designed Influence and Impact Right Where You Are. An Oklahoma gal by birth, Ronne now lives in the Texas Hill Country with her family and rescue pup, Pearl. Connect with Ronne on her website, ronnerock.com, or Instagram.

27

A Pitcher to Pour Out His Love:
Healing Childhood Wounds

By Amanda Schaefer

> *"Therefore, if anyone is in Christ,*
> *he is a new creation.*
> *The old has passed away;*
> *behold, the new has come."*
>
> —
>
> **2 CORINTHIANS 5:17 (ESV)**

In my darkest moment, Jesus came into my life.

Although I grew up attending church, I had never known more than a set of rules—rules that were heavy on top of the ones I already carried from home. Each was like a set of chains around my hands and feet, keeping me in what others found to be the perfect position. But being bound up the way they wanted me left no room for joy.

Despite this, somehow, I have one fragile memory of toddler me underneath the cherry blossom tree. It was a warm and windy moment as I watched tiny pink petals floating in the sky.

Suddenly they began to form a circle in the wind. I can still see them swirling. Without taking the time to think, I began to spin too. My arms stretched out like an airplane, my tiny little dress opening up as if it were blooming to circle the tiny feet below. Feet that longed to dance, skip and run. If only they could take me to a place where I could be free.

It's funny that this beautiful little memory found a way to remain when so many heavy and hurtful ones learned to disappear deep within my heart, to a place they would remain for years.

Throughout my life, I felt like a flower closing, returning back to the tightly formed bud on a stem, instead of effortlessly blooming. To open wide would mean to let the hidden and hard feelings escape. And I just knew that if they left me, it would be with a roar so loud the entire world would shake!

No, these things were meant to live in darkness because that is what they were made of. Dark, tortuous moments where other people's needs overshadowed mine. Moments of abuse and trauma. Moments of injury and woundedness. Moments better left in the darkness.

It's a wonder that I made it through life long enough to meet Jesus. I was so well hidden from the world that I never thought He or anyone else could ever truly see me. I learned to camouflage myself carefully so I would fit in. What others saw was a façade and no one, even I, had truly met the "me" I was born to be. No one but the One who created me, that is.

I know now that God formed me for a purpose. He gave me specific talents and dreams. But life had lied to me one person at a time. Years of emotional damage, trauma and fear had obscured God's original design. But the Creator's blueprints were written with indelible ink. He did not forget what He had planned for me. He loved what He had formed inside my mother's womb. My little life had a plan and a purpose.

That purpose would prove to be bigger and stronger than any of the injustices sent against it.

Looking back, I can see Jesus in every memory, even when I was paralyzed with fear. His kindness and love were with me. And even though

I gave in to the relentless moments that did their best to reform me, somehow the core of my being never became marred.

Cannot the Potter decide what He is making? And even if outer influences pull at the clay, He is able to throw it back on the wheel and make from its essence an even more beautiful vessel to carry His presence and purpose.

The day I believed I was utterly lost and completely defeated is the day I heard the voice of Christ. In agreement with my need for Him and in desperate acceptance of His deity and His love for me, I fully came alive.

He set me to spinning there on the wheel again. I felt the gentle touch of Jesus stretching and forming me in ways I couldn't comprehend. There were pieces of me that He removed because, under closer inspection, they weren't part of my original purpose; they were adornments that the world and the enemy had so desperately tried to leave in me.

There was one particular mark, like a stamp claiming the artist's name, that Jesus spent most of His time working on. Jesus took a bowl of living water and dipped his hand deep inside. Then, as I spun and twirled on the wheel, He applied the water. That memory of spinning under the cherry blossoms rose to the surface of my heart. I rejoiced with the innocence of a child as He worked.

The water smoothed the stamp of the counterfeit artisan into an unblemished surface. And when He was finished, pleased with the final result, Jesus took me from the wheel and into His hands. Instead of trying to stamp me with a mark of His ownership, He gently asked me if I wanted to follow Him. I never said yes more quickly and with so much gratitude.

"Yes, I choose you, Jesus," I said, and as I did, He marked me with something completely unexpected. He marked me with a kiss. The indentation on my vessel looked exactly like a heart, and I carry it with me still to this day.

Later, He placed me in a kiln that felt like a fiery furnace. I experienced times when He refined parts of me to take out the dross. It hurt, but not like those things when I was young. He purposed the refining marks to produce something beautiful, holy and pure. From what seemed like a lost and broken failure, someone who had been depressed, anxious and numb became a Bible teacher, author, speaker and global podcast host who daily shares the love of Jesus.

I am a living example of God's faithfulness and love.

In Japanese culture, when a piece of pottery is broken, artists repair it with gold. It is called *kintsugi*. Instead of throwing the broken vessel away, they highlight and enhance the broken places, creating a stunning piece of art. The name of the process means "golden repair."

When I took the time to look at myself through Jesus-colored glasses, I noticed the artfulness of His work.

He fashioned glorious golden joining in my most traumatic breaks and added jewels around the heart from Jesus' kiss. I was stronger and larger and shaped quite differently. A marred and broken cup was now a pitcher with beauty and purpose. Big enough to fill many cups. I bore the veiny golden scars that had been transformed into purpose.

I came to know that my purpose has always been to have my identity in Christ. No matter what adversity happened to me, He was able to transform it. In His hand, I am now a pitcher that He uses to pour out His love.

Amanda Schaefer is a podcast host, author and speaker. She carries with her the goodness of looking through a lens of gratitude. Her global podcast, A Cup of Gratitude, currently reaches 98 countries and 1700 cities. As a speaker, Amanda teaches the Bible while challenging audiences to live the way that God intends. She has a way of making scripture come alive through everyday examples. Amanda's books include *Crumbled: A Place for Broken People* and *Daily Instaration*. Her books are down-to-earth and packed with biblical truth. Connect with Amanda at acupofgratitude.org, Facebook and Instagram.

28

Learning to Pray Mountain-Moving Prayers

By Jenn Soehnlin

"Have faith in God. I tell you the truth,
you can say to this mountain, '
May you be lifted up and thrown into the sea,'
and it will happen."

—

MARK 11:22-23 (NLT)

I learned about the mountains God could move one evening after Bible study when I was going through one of the hardest seasons of my life.

After our Bible study discussion, our leader asked for prayer requests. My mind swirled with the challenges and doubts and anxieties I was experiencing. I had so many prayer requests, I didn't even know where to start, so I usually kept my requests to myself or kept them at surface level. I was tired of praying for circumstances to change and mountains to move and watching nothing happen. I was tired of feeling like God was silent and far away when I needed Him most. Maybe, just maybe, He would answer the prayers of these sweet ladies in my Bible study group.

And so, before I even knew what I was doing, I shared everything that had been weighing on my soul and my mind for the last few years. The multiple diagnoses of both my sons. The challenges of meeting all their extra needs and their never-ending appointments to help them learn to do what came effortlessly to most children. My wrestling with why a good God would create and give me two children with special needs. My questioning if God wasn't answering my desperate prayers because my faith wasn't strong enough.

After it all came spilling out, I looked at my hands clasped tightly in my lap, ashamed of the doubts and struggles I had dared to speak aloud. I feared their reaction to my vulnerability and yet yearned for God to move through one of these women.

I will never forget what happened next. Without anyone saying a word, each woman abandoned her chair and Bible study materials, and they all gathered around me. Each of them laid a hand on me and they took turns praying over me.

Warm, salty tears spilled down my cheeks and splattered onto my jeans as I listened to the prayers of these women. I honestly don't remember one thing that was prayed over me that night, but what stands out so clearly is that every single woman incorporated scripture into her prayer.

Each woman took a turn boldly declaring the Word of God over me, my anxiety, my doubts, my faith, my struggles, my children and my marriage. Scriptures they had memorized—and perhaps even clung to in their own moments of need—were infused into their prayers and claimed over me and my faith and my family.

Cocooned by the hands, love and prayers of these women, I felt my storm of emotions, anxieties and doubts dissipate.

As the women finished their prayers and I joined them in their final "amen," I realized my weeping had changed from tears of grief and shame to those of joy, hope, thankfulness and freedom.

I felt the power, peace and love of God at that moment. I experienced the power of praying Scripture and the power of praying together in a community. And I wanted to experience that power and peace and love for the rest of my life.

I was so moved by the way those women included Bible verses in their prayers for me that I was determined to learn to do the same. I devoured books about praying scripture.

The Bible became a new treasure trove of possibilities to expand my prayer life and my faith. I looked up scriptures to pray for the things nearest to my heart. Scriptures to pray for my marriage and my husband. Scriptures I could pray for my children. Scriptures to pray for our health, for our home, for our church, for our nation.

I had prayed and prayed that God would heal my sons and restore my faith. Instead of healing my boys, He began teaching me—through my newfound practice of praying scripture—a lot about faith and prayer and special needs parenting. He helped me to see that my children weren't broken or in need of healing, but that they were "fearfully and wonderfully made" (Psalm 139:14 NIV) and had so much to offer the world around them. He taught me a lot about His will and His goodness, the power of praying Scripture, living in an authentic community and so much more.

Yes, God can move the mountains we ask Him to move. Prayers are prayed and then bodies are healed, souls saved and needs met in miraculous ways that could only be orchestrated by God. He was and still is a mountain-moving God.

But I've learned that the mountains God moves are often the ones in our hearts and mindsets.

And God moving those mountains—changing the terrain of our hearts and minds as our will is aligned with His will—is just as miraculous.

Jenn Soehnlin is a mother of two boys who are precious blessings and who both have special needs. She loves spending time with her family, curling up with a good book and a cup of coffee, enjoying a walk through nature and writing. She is the author of Embracing This Special Life and writes about faith, praying Scripture, special needs parenting and more at www.embracing.life. Connect with Jenn on Facebook and Instagram at Jenn Embracing Life.

29

How God Healed My Heart from the Wound of Betrayal:

The Power of Forgiveness

By Hadassah Treu

> *"If he has done you any wrong*
> *or owes you anything, charge it to me."*
>
> —
>
> **PHILEMON 1:18 (NIV)**

W hen my best friend of over 20 years dumped me all of a sudden (at least for me) with the words, "I put an end to our friendship"—refusing to give an explanation or a chance to talk it out—my heart stopped beating and I could hardly breathe. It was incomprehensible to me.

Why? Why would she do this? I held this friendship in very high esteem because we were also sisters in Christ, and there was a strong spiritual bond between us. We prayed for each other daily, and we shared our intimate struggles. We broke the bread of God's Word together and shared meals and moments, and our lives.

However, the unthinkable happened. She pushed me out of her life without a chance for reconciliation. Every time I passed by her house, I thought, *I will never enter this house again or share a meal and a hearty conversation with her*. This thought made me struggle to breathe, bringing tears to my eyes.

For days and months, I would replay internally our last words and lead imaginary dialogues with her. The betrayal and all its consequences were draining my energy, making me sick. This painful experience rocked my world and shook the foundations of my self-confidence and trust in people.

The despair and agony, and the desire for some miraculous reconciliation and self-vindication, drove me to my knees in prayer and to my Bible. I prayed for understanding, wisdom and healing. I asked for the grace and the power to forgive and accept the death of our relationship.

As a believer of many years, I knew very well about God's instruction to forgive. Actually, it is a command, not an instruction. If we love God and want to obey Him, we need to forgive others (friends and family alike). I have forgiven many offenses, hurtful deeds, and words in my life, like abusive behavior and mistreatment in various forms. But I never thought forgiving this betrayal or what I perceived as a betrayal would be so difficult. Perhaps the reason was that the blow came from a loved one.

Nevertheless, the Lord led me persistently toward forgiveness. The Holy Spirit talked to me with the letter to Philemon. First, He urged me to look for the meaning of the name Philemon, which means "he who shows kindness when mistreated." This went straight to the point! But then the Lord continued with the name of sister Apphia, which is mentioned in the second verse. Her name means "she who shields, pure woman."

The Lord showed me He acknowledged my hurt, but He also gently nudged me to take care of my heart. Forgiveness would help me maintain a pure and loving heart that could extend grace and kindness despite the hurt. As always, God showed me that the condition of my heart was of the highest value to Him.

The Holy Spirit also illuminated this verse for me and planted it in my heart: "If he has done you any wrong or owes you anything, charge it to me" (Philemon 1:18 NIV). It was as if the Lord was saying to me, "Forgive her and accept her because of Me. Charge the wrong she has done you to Me. I will repay you. Surrender this to Me."

I followed God's instructions and stuck to my decision to forgive, even and especially when the painful emotions would surface and threaten to overwhelm me. The more I persisted in my choice to forgive and let go, the more God was able to illuminate my heart and mind and bring comfort, healing and restoration.

But, I thought, *how am I supposed to handle my painful emotions?*

Learning to Lament

A powerful step in the process of healing the wound of betrayal was learning to lament. I knew theoretically about the spiritual discipline of lament, but this betrayal forced me to practice lamenting.

Lamenting includes identifying and naming our losses and expressing the painful feelings connected with them. It is mourning in the presence of the Lord, acknowledging that He is with us, He listens and He cares.

The Bible contains a lot of psalms of lament, and one I turned to often was Psalm 55, where the psalmist addresses his pain of the betrayal of a friend:

> *"If an enemy were insulting me, I could endure it;*
> *if a foe were rising against me, I could hide. But it is you,*
> *a man like myself, my companion, my close friend,*
> *with whom I once enjoyed sweet fellowship at the house of God,*
> *as we walked about among the worshipers."*
>
> —
>
> **PSALM 55:12-14 (NIV)**

I could not better express it!

But it is not enough just to pour out our pain. We need to move further and declare our trust in the Lord, following the example of the psalmist:

"As for me, I call to God, and the LORD saves me."

—

PSALM 55:16 (NIV)

I made my own declarations of trust: "God loves me. I choose to trust the reason this happened. I trust His plan and purpose!"

I often accompanied these declarations of trust with prayers for God's vindication, defense and justice, as in Psalms 7 and 9.

The Holy Spirit led me to a daily decision not to give up, even without the chance of reconciliation. I could do this because our Lord is the Lord of resurrection and restoration. He has overcome death, and He surely helped me overcome the death of my relationship with my friend.

Hadassah Treu is an international Christian author, blogger, and poet, the Encouraging Blogger Award Winner for 2020. She loves to encourage people to grow spiritually by applying biblical truths in their lives. Hadassah is a regular contributor to the faith-based platforms Devotable and Koinonia and a contributing author to several award-winning devotional and poetry anthologies. She is also COMPEL Proverbs 31 Ministries Blog writer and Freelancing Community Group leader. Hadassah has been featured on (In)courage, Proverbs 31 Ministries, Her View From Home, Living by Design Ministries, Thoughts About God, Aletheia Today, Today's Christian Living, and other popular sites. Connect with Hadassah at onthewaybg.com and on social media @ onthewaybg and @hadassahtreu.

30

When We Don't Like God's Plans

By Erin Ulerich

"... all the days ordained for me were written in your book before one of them came to be."

—

PSALM 139:16 (NIV)

"Come on, start working!" I pleaded with the Tylenol I had just given my baby girl and prayed it would stop what was happening. Instead, her fever rose. My sweet girl went limp. I watched her slip into a seizure. And there wasn't anything I could do to stop it.

Maggie's first seizure happened right after her first birthday. I didn't know what to do, and that 911 call was honestly an equal mix of praying, cussing and flipping out. My youngest daughter, Ellen, was 18 months old when she had her first seizure. And, although I knew what to do then, the shock of it still rocked me to my core.

Having daughters with a seizure disorder meant that a seizure could happen in the middle of any given day when we least expected it. Each time it happened, I felt as if a rug had been yanked out from under me, and I hit the ground hard. For every one of their seizures, I would experience about two weeks of brain fog and an amazing amount of self-imposed guilt. *It must have been something I did during pregnancy*, I reasoned. I was convinced their seizures were happening because of one of those days when I was too nauseated to choke down that horse pill of a prenatal vitamin.

When we found out that our girls' seizure disorder was genetic, a confusing mix of emotions overwhelmed me. This discovery took the *what-did-I-do-to-cause-this* guilt away, and, at the same time, placed me in a predicament. If this was genetic, then that meant that the Lord chose this for my girls. This seizure disorder was part of His plan as He formed them within me. He purposely chose this path for them. For us.

What do you do when you don't like what God has planned?

Epilepsy had not been in my plans as I pictured motherhood, as I registered at my favorite stores and designed the girls' scrapbooks. It wasn't on my radar as I felt their sweet kicks in my growing belly, reassuring me that everything was fine. In Maggie's baby book, I wrote out the words of Psalm 139:16 in pretty handwriting, not knowing how much I would wrestle with their meaning: "*... all the days ordained for me were written in your book before one of them came to be.*" My own words following the verse radiated trust that I did not yet feel: *From conception to your last breath, your life is in God's hands.*

The Lord and I did some late-night wrestling during these years. If I didn't trust God's plans, what did I trust? Was I counting on finding the solution in the information I gathered about the seizure disorder that had interrupted our lives? Was I trusting my ability to detect a fever and give Tylenol at the right time to avoid seizures?

As I read the Bible, the question in my heart was *can I trust You with my girls?* As a believer, I knew I was supposed to trust God, but I was having a hard time actually trusting Him. I was angry at Him for bringing this into our lives. And I got really honest with Him. I ugly cried, I yell-prayed and I spilled the anger and despair onto the pages of my journals.

The more honest I got with God, the fewer layers there were between us. Layers I had built over the years. He kept leading me back to His Word, the place where I could find His words about Himself. The more I got to know Him, the more I began to trust Him.

In this wrestling, God didn't answer my "why" questions with reasons or explanations. Instead, He opened my eyes to see His faithfulness to my girls and how He provided everything they needed. He showed me that He was worthy of my trust. And, over time, I let go of the things I was trusting in and turned to God with open hands. "I still don't understand," I told Him, "But I trust You with my girls."

Is there something in your life that you didn't see coming — a career change, a diagnosis or the personality traits of your children? Maybe the brokenness of this world just crashed over you out of nowhere, and you can't get your head above water long enough to catch your breath. My friend, you are not alone.

When we are hurting, our first response is to run away from God. But the answers are not there. Run toward truth, read God's Word and wrestle with Him. The process of getting to know Him and finding Him trustworthy is worth going through. No matter what you are facing or how lost you feel, these words are true: *From conception to your last breath, you are in God's hands.* His hands are strong enough to hold you up and gentle enough to guide you back to Him, closer than before.

Erin Ulerich lives, writes and wrangles her three teens in French Camp, Mississippi, a small community beside the historic Natchez Trace Parkway. She has been married to her college sweetheart, Stephen, for 30 years. Erin enjoys laughing with friends, 80s music, chocolate/coffee combinations, and using the latest teen words in the cringiest way possible. Erin is the author of two books: In Unexpected Ways: Christmas in Everyday Life, whose devotions describe how "God with us" is true in our everyday lives, and The Hope of the Helpless: Seven Days of Praying for Orphans. Connect with Erin at erinulerich.com or on social media @ErinUlerich.

31

Sailing the Ship to Transformation

By Cecille Valoria

"Love is patient and kind;
love does not envy or boast;
it is not arrogant or rude.
It does not insist on its own way;
it is not irritable or resentful;
it does not rejoice at wrongdoing,
but rejoices with the truth.
Love bears all things, believes all things,
hopes all things, endures all things."

—

1 CORINTHIANS 13:4-7 (ESV)

Our past minister, like many others, began his sermons with a prayer. The words he routinely included in his prayer—"Thank you, Father, that You love us just the way we are but love us too much to leave us the way we are"—made an indelible impression on me.

Romans 5:8 tells us, "God shows his love for us in that while we were still sinners, Christ died for us" (ESV). Certainly, God accepts us as we are, yet He also readies us for our eternal home with Him. Our life here on earth is the practice arena He provides.

Although our salvation is certain, the battle between our sinful nature and our obedience to God is still a daily struggle. The decisions we make affect our connection with God and our relationships with others.

The moment I accepted Jesus in my life—over 40 years ago—I tried to live according to His example. I immersed myself in scripture, attended Bible studies, served at church, and developed healthy relationships with people. I was proud of how well I thought I had done.

But God.

God looks beyond our deeds or physical appearances and sees the condition of our hearts. Ever gently, through various trials and testing, He chiseled off some of my worldly ways. He revealed what was in my heart and what He needed to hollow out of my heart. Recently, He made me aware of what that was when He asked me to be the full-time caretaker of my 94-year-old dad. I call it my "Jonah Experience."

Taking care of someone is a complex endeavor, and I was given a double dose of it. Besides taking care of my dad, I was attending to my brother's needs. He lived in a nursing home three hours away. I knew I couldn't fulfill this Herculean task with my own strength and ability, but only through the power of the Holy Spirit and God's constant presence in my life.

Like Jonah, I initially sailed on the ship of reasoning and evading, taking me to my own Tarshish of excuses. *I am teaching full-time. I don't know if we are financially ready for me to retire. I'm not sure how to meet the needs of an elderly individual.*

Finally, in June 2020, the inevitable happened. According to God's perfect plan, I embarked on the journey of caring for my father.

However, unlike Jonah's ship, tossed in the stormy seas before he yielded in obedience to God's call, I felt a tumultuous turmoil within me after I said yes to my dad and God. I often knelt in prayer, crying out and begging God for guidance, wisdom and the strength to carry on. I asked God for a constant filling of His Holy Spirit and steadfast love for my dad to sustain me through the journey.

I was certain I had a deep love for him. Like clockwork, I used to call and check on him and my mom daily, telling them each time that I loved them.

As I navigated through waves of a myriad of emotions, I felt God's steadfast presence. He directed me to anchor myself in His Word. God opened my eyes to what loving someone truly meant.

He taught me—love was not just in words but by what I did, motivated by a pure heart. He ferried me through the waters of my new reality, employing 1 Corinthians 13:4-7 to be my compass.

As times of struggle, overwhelming needs and weariness enveloped me, God made me understand that love keeps on going, even when all I wanted to do was run away and give up. "Love is patient and kind" (v.4).

When dementia slowly manifested in my dad, causing him to demand that things be done his way, and I wanted to impose my own, God reminded me that love "does not insist on its own way" (v.5).

When I felt sorry for myself for being the only one shouldering the responsibilities to care for both my brother and dad, God whispered, "love does not envy or boast" (v. 4); "it is not irritable or resentful" (v.5).

When all I wanted was to lash out in anger at twisted, hurtful words spoken against me, God made me remember: "Love bears all things, believes all things, hopes all things, endures all things" (v.7).

Furthermore, He repeatedly reminded me to "be quick to hear, slow to speak, slow to anger" (James 1:19 ESV).

I prayed, repented, persevered, rejoiced and praised God. Prayed. Repented. Persevered. Rejoiced. Praised God.

Have I completely learned what love truly is and how to love as He loves? No.

My journey with God is far from over. But I know that how I love now is so much better than the way I loved before.

Is God calling you to let go of something or take a leap of faith to do something? Is the ship of doubt, fear or insecurity moving you away from His presence and restraining you from heeding His call?

Take courage! Sail on the ship of transformation with Him. God does not leave us on our own. He indwells us with the Holy Spirit to enable us to live our earthly lives according to His divine will and purpose. There is nothing too difficult for Him. He braces those He beckons to partner with Him.

Cecille Valoria is a Christian author, blogger, podcaster and retired schoolteacher. She finds expression in her passion for discipling and encouraging others through devotional writing, her blog and her podcast, Digging Deep for Treasures with Cecille Valoria. She founded the nonprofit, A Simple Touch Ministry, which delivers flowers to patients. Cecille also published a memoir, *Slaying Your Fear Giants: Moving from a Jungle of Terror to a Garden of Peace*, which chronicles her battle with anxiety and God's healing and faithfulness. Cecille's writing is featured in various anthologies and ministries. She currently has two children's picture book manuscripts waiting to be published. Connect with Cecille on her website, cecillevaloria.com, podcast or Instagram.

32

Sharing Struggles to Help Others:
One Exceptional Life
By Wendy Wallace

I like to refer to myself as the most positive and happy quadruple amputee that you'll ever meet, and I'm living One Exceptional Life.

I'm a passionate believer that everything is overcomeable. My mission is to help other women rediscover God's joy, peace and fulfillment amid the trials of life by walking more closely with God.

My story is about the power of prayer, faith, hope, and overcoming, to find and carry out God's will for my life. I was not supposed to survive. My doctors said there was no chance. But my husband told them, "You don't know my God and what He is capable of." The prayers of family, friends, and even strangers, who had the faith that God would answer those prayers, changed the course of my illness and showed those doctors just Who has the power over life and death.

Living With Limitations

Have you ever had a time when your life was turned completely upside down?

Let me take you back to a time that, although I'd rather forget, became a passage that changed my life in so many ways. And it put me on a course to find God's will for my life and use it as a springboard to serving Him by serving others.

One minute I was at home in bed with what I thought was a case of the flu. The next minute, it was actually three weeks later. I was awake from my coma and lying in a hospital bed with bandages where both hands and both feet had been.

I had developed necrotizing fasciitis, a deadly and rapidly spreading flesh-eating disease. Doctors had to perform multiple surgeries, finally amputating my hands and feet to save my life.

The first thing I remember thinking was, "Lord, how am I going to do this? How can I ever live a normal life like this?" You would think I would've been petrified, but I felt peace. I was no longer in danger, and I was safe in the arms of Jesus. My favorite verses came to mind, and the Lord reminded me that if I trusted Him, we would get through things together.

But later, despair took over. After three months in the hospital and rehab, I came home in a wheelchair, wondering how I could still be a wife and a mom to three teenagers that they needed me to be. I was sad and frustrated, and I wondered what it all meant. Most of all I just couldn't figure out what I was going to do with myself for the rest of my life. The kids were growing up and moving out, and my husband worked all day. How would I spend my days? Frankly, I was stuck in my pity party!

Over the next several years, I dug into the Word of God to grow my faith and to figure out why bad things happen to us. I did Bible studies on my own and in church. We reasoned together as the Bereans did in the Book of Acts. I questioned God: "Is there something I did that this punishment is for?"

Ultimately, I learned that our struggles don't always happen because of the things that we do. But possibly others need to learn from our experiences. And in my case, it wasn't until the timing was right that I would learn that lesson.

Finding a New Purpose

One day, my daughter Megan approached me with what she thought was a great idea. She invited me to go river tubing with her! I thought, *what kind of crazy sense does it make, to put a woman with no hands and no feet in a tube and push her down the river?* But I agreed, and that event was the turning point in my life.

You see, up until then, I used the word "can't" for so many things. I just didn't think I was capable. And I used my disabilities as an excuse to avoid trying to do the things that ordinarily I would have loved to do. But that day in the river was one of my best days since my amputations. Because it proved to me that I was far more capable than I was giving myself credit for.

Prior to that, many people had encouraged me to share my story by writing a book or a blog. I always declined because I didn't know where to start. But that day in the river, we decided to share my experiences with the hope that other people might be stuck the way I was, and just maybe I could offer some encouragement.

The next day, One Exceptional Life was born. I shared my stories of life as an amputee. But I really thrived in sharing tips and tools for growing spiritually, overcoming challenges and finding joy, gratitude and positivity in everything. The response I got was overwhelming; I heard from people around the world, telling me I encouraged them in their own struggles and inspired them to be more intentional with Bible study and prayer.

In that response, I understood why I had to go through my illness, my amputations and my pity party. Because other women just like me are struggling with life and need encouragement. So when I read 2 Corinthians 1:3–4 (KJV), it all made sense:

> *"Blessed be God, even the Father of our Lord Jesus Christ, the Father of mercies, and the God of all comfort; Who comforteth us in all our tribulation, that we may be able to comfort them which are in any trouble, by the comfort wherewith we ourselves are comforted of God."*

Over the last four-and-a-half years I have continued to share articles of inspiration, as well as my services as a Christian living coach, to help folks who need the reminder that a closer walk with God—and growing their faith, gratitude, joy and positivity—will bring them fulfillment and a peace that passes understanding.

We all struggle! Some experiences are more life-changing than others. It's what you do with your situation that matters. Listen to the wisdom from Proverbs 3: When you trust in the Lord with all your heart and lean not on your own understanding of the situation, but instead, acknowledge Him and His ways, seeking His guidance through prayer, with thanksgiving, He will direct your paths ... if you let Him.

We don't always understand why bad things have to happen. But we do know "that all things work together for good to them that love God, to them who are the called according to his purpose" (Romans 8:28 KJV).

Wendy Wallace is a wife, mom, Christian coach, inspiration blogger, digital product creator and author. She is also a quadruple amputee. She loves spending time with her family, playing with flowers and eating lots of ice cream. You can find her at One Exceptional Life, where she helps women rediscover God's joy, peace and fulfillment amid the trials of life by becoming more intentional with God. Wendy has two eBooks: *From Struggle to Joy: Biblical Comfort for Finding Peace in Life's Challenges* and *Victory Over Affliction: 30 Mindset Challenges to Motivate You.* Connect with Wendy on her blog, Facebook, LinkedIn or Pinterest.

33

My Security Blanket:

Letting Go by Embracing Jesus

By Dawn Ward

"Bankie! Bankie!" Ignoring my cries, my parents hurriedly packed our car with suitcases and snacks, placed me in the back seat and said their goodbyes before departing. After spending a few weeks visiting family in South Dakota, they were eager to get on the road to head back home. Already running late and racing against sundown, they could not waste another minute searching for my missing blanket.

"Don't worry about Dawn's blanket," Aunt Rita shouted to Mom as she waved goodbye. "It's around here somewhere. I will find it and mail it to your house. It will probably show up right about the time you pull into the driveway." Mom, cautiously optimistic, breathed a sigh of relief. "You're right. Anyway, she will forget all about it once we are on the road."

"Bankie! Bankie!" A hundred miles into our trip, my two-year-old mind was still fixated on what it wanted most—the comfort of my blanket. By now, we had traveled too far to turn back and retrieve my missing treasure. Mom's attempts to distract me only made matters worse. As I grew more inconsolable, my father became more agitated, and my mother more frustrated.

Desiring a break from the summer heat and relief from my constant whining, my parents kept their eyes open for the nearest rest stop. Sighting one, they prepared to pull over. Checking the review mirror, Dad noticed a car speeding behind them. Seconds later, he caught sight of a woman hanging out the passenger window with what appeared to be a flag flying over her head. Aunt Rita!

"Well, I'll be!" Dad's words trailed off and, with a big smile, he pointed for Mom to take a look. Wide-eyed and shaking her head in disbelief, she yelled, "Bankie! Bankie!" Moments later, I was joyfully reunited with my long, lost blankie.

While I was too young at the time to remember this story, my mother and aunt loved to retell it for many years to come. What made it especially fascinating was not that I could throw a fit that lasted over 100 miles. It wasn't even that my aunt and uncle, upon finding my blanket, drove such a long distance to return it to me.

I find it interesting that it took my parents so long to recognize the speeding car behind them. It turns out that my relatives, on their blankie-returning expedition, left their home only a few minutes after our departure. While not quite able to catch up to us, they drove down the highway with our tail lights in sight for several miles before Dad finally caught a view of them in the distance. Help had arrived minutes earlier. My parents were simply too upset and preoccupied to notice.

Years later, after retiring my worn-out blanket, I still longed for the feeling of security it brought me. Because of my father's excessive drinking, our home could be quite volatile, and I often heard my parents arguing with each other. Never knowing what mood they would come home in, I worried a lot and became a very anxious child. No longer finding comfort in a worn-out piece of cloth, I developed certain coping skills to give me the security I longed for. The comfort measures I carried with me into adulthood were behaviors such as people-pleasing, perfectionism, staying hypervigilant and being a control freak.

As a child, I was taught the Lord always watches over us, but as an adult with children of my own, I could not shake the feeling that if I didn't protect them, no one else would. I clung to scriptures assuring me of the Lord's presence and tried to trust him, but I still couldn't release the burden I was carrying for their safety and well-being.

Enter addiction. Growing up in an atmosphere of fear and uncertainty, I vowed to keep our children safe and our home free of alcohol and drugs. We sent our kids to Christian school, attended church, vetted their friends and parents, and watched their every move. Despite our best efforts, addiction made its way into our family, and we discovered our middle son was using drugs.

The walls of the fortress I had built to keep our home secure came tumbling down. I longed to reach for my security blanket, but it was long gone. Instead, I rushed into battle, donning my super-mom cape, fully armed with strategies to save him, plus some trusty coping skills to guard my heart.

Fast-forward a few years. With God's grace and plenty of hard work, our boy had finally beaten his addiction. Removing my battle-worn cape, I breathed a sigh of relief. *Whew*, I thought. *I can finally retire this old thing once and for all.*

But the enemy was not satisfied to leave well enough alone. Once again, addiction crept into our family, moving from one son to the next. I coped the only way I knew how—by grabbing my battle-worn cape and running to the rescue. My desire to help turned into an obsession as I fixated on fixing him. As if on replay 24/7, the words repeated in my head: *You have to save him. You have to fix him.* My prayers became desperate pleas for God to help my son.

Never once did it occur to me to pray for myself.

As my fear intensified, my faith dwindled. Where once I was blanketed in the Lord's comfort and assurance, now I was cloaked with a mantle of misery and dejection. I wanted to take off my super-mom cape and release my son to the Lord. I just didn't know how. The only way I knew to cope was to keep fighting with all my might.

Until one day, when a conversation took place that turned it all around. My husband, discerning it was time to intervene, spoke these words of truth to me: "You are going to worry yourself to death." In tears, I whispered, "You're right. You have permission to write them on my tombstone. 'She Worried Herself to Death.'"

No sooner did the words leave my mouth when I heard the Lord speak quietly, yet firmly, "No. I want them to read, 'She Trusted God.'"

Just then, a blanket of warmth enveloped me as Jesus gently removed this weary momma's worn-out cape, pulled me close and nestled me under the shadow of his wings. Like my blankie-bearing relatives on that long, dusty road so many years ago, help had arrived. In fact, it had been there all along. I was just too upset and preoccupied to notice.

With a sigh of relief, I let go of the old cape and grabbed the hem of Jesus' garment as I confidently whispered, "She trusts God."

Dawn Ward is a speaker, writer and biblical life coach. She is the founder of The Faith to Flourish, a ministry that equips women with addicted loved ones to break free from the cycle of addiction, reclaim their lives, and flourish in their faith.

Dawn is the co-author of the book "Still Standing After All the Tears Workbook: Faith in the Battle Edition and a contributing author for the devotional, Shepherd on Duty. She is currently in the process of writing her first solo book, *From Guilt to Grace: Freedom and Healing for Christian Moms of Addicted Children* (ETA first quarter 2024).

Dawn has been married to her husband, Steve, for over forty years and is a mom to three adult children. It is her passion to help women grow in their faith as they learn to understand the Bible and apply it to their lives. Connect with Dawn at The Faith to Flourish on most social media platforms.

34

God is Good, Even When We Fall Short:

Exchanging Performance for Presence

By Nicole Williams

*"And remember,
I am with you always,
to the end of the age."*

—

MATTHEW 28:20 (NRSVUE)

While the winter wind whipped at the windows, my father's roaring laughter filled the room as he looked across the table at me. It felt like everyone was watching. "You should be a lawyer, Nicole. You've always wanted people to see things your way."

My heart skipped. My dad's magnetic presence overpowered everything else. With just a word from him, I believed anything was possible.

He believed I could sail solo in the San Francisco Bay when I was 11, run a marathon at 12, translate for our family in a foreign country, work two jobs to pay for college and be accepted into law school. His faith helped me believe I could accomplish what I set my mind to. He believed, so I did too.

I stood on my porch in Austin, waving goodbye after seeing him for the weekend. We were both smiling. It would be the last time I would ever see him. The next day he would die in a car accident, almost 2,000 miles away. I couldn't quite grasp the truth of my mom's words when she called me. Time wouldn't move; I kept picturing him from my porch, smiling at me through the windshield as he drove away. I was 21 and about to start my last year of college.

A Devastating Loss

Disappointment has a way of boldly arriving on our doorstep and thinks nothing of lurking like an unwelcome visitor. Though it's easy to miss its approach, we never miss its arrival.

When you lose a parent at a young age, it feels like you're suddenly jumping between stones on a roaring river. Life decisions that used to feel collaborative now felt ominously weighty. I lost my footing on one of those jumps and disappointed myself. A dream I shared with my dad drifted away, and I felt like the last thing connecting us was gone.

Three years after my dad died, I found myself in law school thousands of miles from home and facing the darkest time in my life. Well into my fourth semester, I felt overcome by a depression I had never known. It was debilitating. I was overwhelmed, broken and lost; I didn't think I would ever believe in myself again. Among so many classmates, I felt terminally alone. For so many years, I was equipped by the faith of my dad, but he was gone.

God used my mom and a therapist to save my life. My mom, who had always been in my dad's shadow, said four words: "You can come home." She believed in something different than my dad—that I was whole regardless of performance. She heard my hurt and saw my loss, and showed me I was loved, just as I was. Her unconditional agape love and therapy kept my head above water long enough for hope to return.

Sometimes life brings us devastation, and in the interest of minimizing hurt, we choose to be perpetually prepared for loss. We think, *If I can just keep my expectations low, no one can hurt me—even myself.*

But there's a problem with this: it sets our hearts in a state of distrusting God. Instead of fully believing in God's goodness, grace, mercy, love, faithfulness, kindness and gentleness, we minimize our faith in Him. By never really believing that life can be magnificent, we guard ourselves against being let down. And when we do this, rather than being ready to fly, we're ready for the worst and fully expecting it.

Living like that is a tragedy.

The Power of Self-Forgiveness

I never expected to drop out of law school. I had always finished everything I started. When we're the source of our own loss, the inability to let go forms a snare. We won't let ourselves forget because we're more practiced at giving than receiving. Even when we willingly offer grace to other people, knowing this is part of healing and forgiveness, we may struggle to offer the same to ourselves.

It can be hard to forgive ourselves. We may carry disappointment into the next stage of our life. The weight of our story is like a hidden anchor trying to keep us from being free, even if no one else sees it. I know, I've been there. It can be a lifelong struggle.

But what would happen if we set our hearts on lofty goals and genuinely believed in the goodness of God, even if we fell short?

We could let go of "knowing for certain" what our lives will become. Imagine the freedom we could have if we sought to forgive ourselves and others; worked toward peace in our communities; loved our spouse and valued a strong marriage; genuinely trusted God with our children; worked toward reconciled relationships; and simply pursued our dreams.

Imagine that God cares about all these things. Because He does. We might not always get it right, but our hope will be placed in the One whose great love abounds. Countless times I've sensed God looking at me across the table, reminding me of His great love for me, apart from any accomplishments. Even if the path changes and we need to pivot, God's love remains.

My life didn't turn out according to my plans. Did it turn out better? I don't really know; I can only live and experience one life. But I sense the continual rich presence of God when some doors close and others open. I let go of my dad for the hope and glory of an eternal Father; one who would exchange my stone-stepping by parting the sea entirely. It's been in the daily surrender that I experience the wholeness of His presence. And I wouldn't change that for anything.

Nicole Williams is a writer who teaches people how to forgive by creating biblical and practical habits. She's the author of *RISE UP: Believing God When the World is Falling Apart*. Nicole has read through the Bible many times, and her passion is influencing people to read the Bible for themselves. Get her free guide *Start Tiny: 7 Habits to Forgive & Be Free*, and find out when the Forgiveness Course launches by subscribing at msnicolewilliams.com. She lives in Houston with her husband of 29 years and is a mom to two young adults. Connect with Nicole on Instagram @ms.nicolewilliams.

Stories of
Spiritual Transformation

Get to know the authors of Life Changing Stories. Scan the QR code to listen in as they reveal the heart behind their inspiring story.

About the Author

Mary Rooney Armand is a writer, teacher, and creator of the faith-based blog ButterflyLiving.org. Her writing has been featured on multiple Christian websites and she is the author of the book, *Identity, Understanding, and Accepting Who I am in Christ* available on Amazon. This is Mary's second book, a collaboration of 34 amazing authors sharing Life Changing stories.

Besides writing, Mary leads and teaches retreats and small groups. She directed Kids Hope USA, a mentoring program for children, worked in marketing and sales and has led mission trips to Honduras. Mary is a life coach with a Bachelor's degree in Marketing and an MBA. She and her wonderful husband Cory live in Louisiana with their 4 children and 2 dogs!

**More places to read ButterflyLiving's stories
about a transformed life in Christ:**

– Facebook –

www.facebook.com/bfl2022

– Instagram –

www.instagram.com/butterflyliving_

– Twitter –

www.twitter.com/maryrarmand

– On the Web –

www.butterflyliving.org

www.ingramcontent.com/pod-product-compliance
Lightning Source LLC
Chambersburg PA
CBHW051622120626
46551CB00014B/1913